1001
SEXCAPADES
TO DO
IF YOU
DARE

1001

SEXCAPADES
TO DO
IF YOU
DARE

Bobbi Dempsey

Avon, Massachusetts

Published by
Adams Media, an F+W Publications Company
57 Littlefield Street, Avon, MA 02322. U.S.A.
www.adamsmedia.com

ISBN 10: 1-59869-903-2
ISBN 13: 978-1-59869-903-6

Printed in the United States of America.

J I H G F E D C B A

Library of Congress Cataloging-in-Publication Data
is available from the publisher.

This publication is designed to provide accurate and authoritative information with regard to the subject matter covered. It is sold with the understanding that the publisher is not engaged in rendering legal, accounting, or other
professional advice. If legal advice or other expert assistance is required, the
services of a competent professional person should be sought.

—From a *Declaration of Principles* jointly adopted by a Committee of the
American Bar Association and a Committee of Publishers and Associations

Many of the designations used by manufacturers and sellers to distinguish
their product are claimed as trademarks. Where those designations appear in
this book and Adams Media was aware of a trademark claim, the designations
have been printed with initial capital letters.

The publisher and author disclaim any damages or injury resulting from
execution of ideas presented herein.

Interior pattern art © Jamie Farrant/iStockphoto.

This book is available at quantity discounts for bulk purchases.
For information, please call 1-800-289-0963.

CONTENTS

ᴵNTRODUCTION

You want fun and passion in your life, right? Of course, we all do. But then life gets in the way, and we get tired, busy, and just plain uninspired. Before you know it, your love life has gotten stale and those passionate encounters have become a distant memory.

If it's any consolation, you're not alone. It happens to everyone. Even the most creative and adventurous couples eventually run out of ideas—or just run out of steam.

The good news is, you can get that spark back. All it takes is a few new moves—the more daring, the better. That's where this book comes in. No matter what your sexual tastes, you will find many daring suggestions that are sure to get your blood pumping.

Feeling a little shy and nervous? Start off with a few milder moves until you feel ready to unleash your inner wild child. Or, live dangerously and go straight for the high-risk maneuvers.

Each idea can be used on either men or women (though you may see a "he" or "she"), unless you see a specific note that it's geared to one sex or the other. And each item is ranked according to risk and "wildness," which tend to go hand-in-hand. So scan through the book and choose those that are right for you and your partner.

RATINGS KEY

 =
Sexy, but low-risk

 =
A little wilder, but not too crazy

 =
People will envy your sexual adventures

 =
You are a sexual daredevil

 =
It doesn't get any wilder

CHAPTER 1

BEGINNER BASICS

Trying new things can be scary—especially when it comes to your sex life. But wanna know what's even scarier? Letting your libido wither away and die because your sex life has gone from hot to ho-hum. Even if things haven't gotten quite that bad yet, chances are you could still use a little sexual supercharge once in a while. There are few people or couples among us whose sex life is superhot and steamy all the time.

The good news? You don't need to go really wild and crazy (although that would definitely spice things up, and you should try to work your way up to that level—see the suggestions later in this book). By trying even a few new things from this chapter, you can bring the passion back to your sex life—or make it even more passionate than it already is. Yes, it can be intimidating to break out of your comfort zone. That's why you can start out slowly with these simple steps.

1 **SAY SOMETHING SEXY.** Tell your partner you want him or her—now. Make it simple, direct, and to the point. For added effect, sprinkle in some X-rated words. Ideally, say it in a sexy whisper—or a forceful tone that makes it clear you will not take "no" for an answer. Yes, it really is that easy.

2 **OPEN THE DOOR NAKED.** This is a simple yet obvious strategy that really can't be misconstrued or go undetected (unlike more subtle moves). Your partner will usually take it from there. Tip: it's a good idea to peek through the window or a peephole as your partner approaches, just to make sure he hasn't brought along an unexpected guest for dinner.

3 **DO A SNEAK ATTACK.** Sneak up on her naked when she least expects it. (Just use caution if she is near a hot stove or operating dangerous power tools.) Brush up against her, or give her a naughty caress or squeeze. She'll be thrilled at this ambush.

4 **SHARE A BLANKET.** This is a simple yet sexy move that can lead to all kinds of fun. Your hands are free to wander and explore—while safely hidden under the protective camouflage of the blanket. What happens under the covers, stays under the covers.

5 **SET THE STAGE FOR SEXY BEDROOM ANTICS.** A few simple steps to create the perfect atmosphere

can go a long way. Preparation is the key here. Sprinkle the bed with rose petals and surround the room with candles. This romantic setting is the perfect atmosphere for a night to remember.

6 **WALK ON THE BEACH.** Ideally, you should try to find a relatively secluded beach, or at least one that isn't too crowded with noisy families and teenagers. With your toes in the sand and a drink in your hands, a perfect seaside kiss is nature's quintessential recipe for romance.

7 **GET SUDSY IN A SENSUAL WAY.** What better way to unwind after a long day (and pave the way to an enjoyable night) than to share a relaxing bubble bath? Luxuriate in a candlelit tub for two. Lavender- or vanilla-scented bubbles add a soft, yet sweet, aroma as you both relax after a long day.

8 **BUILD A FIRE.** Curl up beside a cozy fire and talk all night. Or, let your bodies do the talking. You can even make your own delicious melted treats. With the passion ablaze, you won't be able to deny your erotic desires. Bearskin rug not included . . .

9 **RELIVE AN X-RATED MEMORY.** Dr. Ava Cadell, founder of *www.loveologyuniversity.com*, shares this idea: Look at your lover and finish this sentence: "The most memorable erotic experience that I have had with you

was . . . " Then re-enact your most erotic experience together even if it's not in the same place.

10 TRADE NIGHTLY FOOT RUBS.   It's easy, it's intimate, and it just makes you feel good. It can be tough to concentrate on anything else when your feet are aching and tired. Soothing a long day's sore feet can lead to an impromptu bedroom romp. Try using some body oil (which you can then put to good use in other ways).

11 ENGAGE IN SILLINESS (AS A GATEWAY TO SEX).   Dr. Cadell also suggests that you "plan to meet at a bar or nightclub. Forget the drinks but do what you want and do engage in a little tomfoolery. The sillier the better! If you're at a bar that has a dance floor, make out like two high school kids! This night is about letting your guard down and having a little fun." At the end of the night, call a cab and take the party home. Every now and again a little harmless sex is just what the doctor ordered.

12 WRITE A STEAMY LOVE LETTER TO YOUR LOVER.   Dr. Cadell shares another wise suggestion: Put a little thought into your letter before sending it on its way. Make your letter as steamy and as sexy as you possibly can. Use plenty of hot adjectives in describing all the things you love most about your partner. Suggest a rendezvous and describe in graphic details what will take place. Make sure you are very specific

with a time and place, the intention of the date, and what your lover might expect. Then spray your love letter with your favorite perfume or cologne to give it that personal touch. Once it's delivered and in your unsuspecting lover's hands, you can expect a big note of thanks, not to mention the rendezvous you create as an unforgettable memory.

13 PLAY THE "NAUGHTY NAME" GAME.   Mary Jo Fay of *www.outoftheboxx.com* says, "There's something fun about naming your body parts . . . particularly the penis and vagina. For example, Captain America and Wonder Woman. Then you can have conversations about these secret characters even when you're having lunch at a business lunch or with your parents. Such as, "Hey, honey, do you think Captain America will be on this afternoon when we get home?" And she replies, "Yeah, I think so. I bet Wonder Woman will be on about the same time. That should be fun!"

14 WHISPER SWEET NOTHINGS.   This is a lost art that should definitely be revived. If you can, come up with something sexy or shocking. Then again, it almost doesn't matter what you say—just having your warm breath near his ear will probably turn him on.

15 WHISPER SWEET NOTHINGS—IN PUBLIC.   Tell your partner—in graphic detail—what you want to do together when you get home. Ignore curious glances of onlookers who are wondering what you're whispering.

For maximum effect, try this when you won't be home for a while, to build the anticipation.

16 **TREAT YOUR PARTNER TO SOME STEAMY SHOWER ACTION, BY SURPRISE.** Your partner is in the bathroom, getting ready for what she thinks will be a typical boring shower. But you've got something better in mind. Wait a minute or two after she gets in the shower, and then slide in with her. When she asks what you're doing, tell her you're conserving water!

17 **LOOK, LISTEN, AND LEARN WHILE YOUR PARTNER PROVIDES AN INTIMATE ROAD-MAP.** Take half an hour each to show one another how and where you want to be touched, with the other looking on to learn. Feel free to take notes (or maybe even pictures) if that will help you remember these important lessons in pleasure.

18 **SEND YOUR PARTNER ROMANTIC GREETINGS AT WORK.** Send a romantic, lurid, or sexy love letter to your partner's office, marked "Personal and Private." Ladies, feel free to add a whiff of your sexiest perfume. Oh, your partner has a nosy secretary who tends to snoop in the mail? Good—be sure to make it extra steamy!

19 **FINGERPAINT . . .** each other. Draw pictures on each other with chocolate syrup. Or, use any other substi-

tute of edible (and, ideally, tasty) material. You can also highlight your partner's most "interesting" areas or write short notes to each other. If you make a mistake, just lick it up.   ♥♥♥

20 **WRITE ON EACH OTHER.**   While naked and lying in bed together, use your fingers to draw letters on your partner's back. You can write anything you want, but spelling out a sexy message will make this more exciting. Try doing it with the lightest possible touch, for a tickling sensation.   ♥♥

21 **WRITE ON—TO THE NEXT LEVEL.**   Spell out a sex act you would like to do to your partner. If you want to make it easier for him to figure out, stick to something you can spell in a few letters. If he can guess what you have written, he gets to enjoy that sex act. ♥♥♥

22 **GET A DVD DEMO.**   Watch a how-to sex tape or DVD together for some ways to break away from the normal! Look into *Kama Sutra* and other unfamiliar territory. See if you can make it through the entire tape without touching each other. (If you can't, don't worry—you can always hit pause!)   ♥♥♥

23 **COOK NAKED.**   Food and sex are the ingredients of a steamy session following a delicious kitchen cookoff. (Just be very careful to avoid anything involving hot grease that might spatter near sensitive areas.) Once

the meal is ready, tickle your senses by feeding each
other . . . blindfolded. ♥♥♥

24 **COP A FEEL.**   Come up with every possible excuse
to touch your partner's private areas. Make it as sexy,
funny, or creative as you like. One idea: tell your man
you need some money, and then reach deep into his
pocket, and touch his manhood. Express your delight
upon discovering what a big wad of cash he has! ♥♥

25 **BE DIRECT.**   Sometimes you just can't rely on hints
and subtle glances to get your message across. If your
man is ignoring you while watching the game (or your
woman is engrossed in her favorite soap), just go up to
him without a word and plant a deep, long kiss on him.
Grab his hand and say, "You. Me. Bedroom." ♥♥♥

26 **BE IMPATIENT.**   You should not be forced to wait
until your partner feels like meeting your needs. After
all, you deserve the top spot on her priority list! If you
try to lead her into the bedroom and she doesn't move
quickly enough, just start groping her right then and
there. Your urgency will surely get her attention. ♥♥

27 **SPEND THE WEEKEND IN BED.**   Want forty-eight
hours of pure bliss? Here are Dr. Cadell's tips: Start by
clearing your schedule. The only work you're going to
be doing over the weekend is pleasing your lover in
between the sheets! It's okay to keep the television
and DVD in the bedroom, but only if you are going to

throw in an adult film to liven things up. Cook breakfast naked in the kitchen and then eat it together in bed. Skip lunch and order takeout for dinner. You can have it delivered to your door as long as you don't frighten the delivery boy by opening the door stark naked.

28 **KISS AND MAKE UP.** They say a good makeup session can almost make a fight worthwhile. In the middle of a fight, call it quits by taking your partner in your arms and engaging in a passionate kiss. Makeup sex could come sooner than you think.

29 **BE SLACKERS.** Give yourself permission to be lazy for one day. Play impromptu hooky from work or school just to enjoy each other. You don't even need to get out of bed at all if you don't feel like it. The one that "sacrifices" the most by staying home gets to start the games.

30 **HAVE LUNCHTIME SEX.** Dr. Cadell suggests having a naughty nooner. "Even if you don't make lunch for your lover, you could try leaving a love note in his or her briefcase. The idea is pretty basic and the plan is simple. Make it hot and steamy. Invite your lover to meet you somewhere private for an afternoon quickie. If going to a motel or hotel is out of the question, you could always arrange to meet at home. The important thing to keep in mind is that this is supposed to be a secret; it's something that the two of

you will have to keep to yourselves. It's a lot like having an affair, only this way you're not cheating on anyone. Plan to make the appointment during the lunch hour while everyone else is out and about. There's an added sense of excitement that comes with knowing that while everyone else is simply enjoying a sandwich and an apple, you're enjoying something much more satisfying."

31 **Have sex first thing in the morning.** Dr. Cadell strongly recommends taking advantage of that morning wood. "Great sex first thing in the morning with your lover? Can you imagine a better way to start your day? A good romp in the sack early in the day will get your heart pumping, but research also shows that sex at any time of the day will also help to keep you looking younger."

32 **Kiss.** A lot. Kissing is often seen as just as prelude to something bigger and better. Appreciate kissing as an exciting experience on its own, not just when you are hoping it will lead to something else. Kiss your partner as often as possible, especially when saying hello or goodbye—but also at random times, just because you feel like it.

33 **Increase the frequency.** Of course, we all know that quality counts when it comes to sex. But let's face it—quantity is important, too. It's an inevitable circle: the more sex you have, the more sex you want.

Avoid long droughts whenever possible, to keep the flame from going out completely. ♥ ♥

34 **ENJOY QUICKIES (ONCE IN A WHILE).** No, you shouldn't try to exist solely on quickies, but at times when a long interlude is out of the question, a quickie can tide you over nicely for awhile. Plus, the occasional fast-and-furious session (no pillow talk necessary) is sometimes all you really need. ♥ ♥ ♥

35 **MAKE LOVE AT MIDNIGHT.** Dr. Cadell says, "Sex in the middle of the night can be an extremely satisfying experience. It works best when you're both still very much asleep, but very willing and easily coerced into having sex. Let your dreams take you further into your sexual fantasy, but allow your body to turn this fantasy into reality. So, ladies: wake your lover up by sliding your tongue up and down his body followed by the caress of your hair, nails, breasts, and your warm, inviting breath. Tell him what you want to do to him in graphic detail and your lover will be putty in your hands." ♥ ♥

36 **GIVE YOUR PARTNER AN X-RATED GIFT.** Dr. Cadell suggests giving your lover a signed, framed photo of your most preferred body part. ♥ ♥ ♥

37 **SPOON.** Simple, right? You'd think so, but many couples seem to keep a world of space between them. That physical distance can quickly morph into emotional distance if you aren't careful. If you start off in a spooning position, it's very likely that things will progress naturally to a sexier level. Sure, eventually (once you are both really ready to go to sleep), you may want your space. But spooning is a great way to start the night.

38 READ A CLASSIC SEX BOOK—TOGETHER. There are lots of great choices—try The *Joy of Sex* or a similar staple of the sexual how-to tomes. You might be surprised at how much "Sex 101" stuff you have forgotten (or never knew in the first place).

39 MAKE A DATE. Who says sex always has to be spontaneous? These days, we all have busy schedules. Sometimes things need to be planned in advance, and sex is no exception. Coordinate your schedules, synchronize your calendars, and set a date that works for both of you. And make sure to keep it at all costs (barring a life-or-death emergency). Bonus: the sweet anticipation will make you more excited when the time finally arrives.

40 FOCUS ON FOREPLAY. Too many couples, especially those that have been together for awhile, skimp on foreplay (or skip it altogether). Yes, the "main attraction" is enjoyable, but it's not the only thing on the menu. Adding more foreplay to your bedroom routine can make sex more satisfying for both of you.

41 Do some dirty dancing.   It is a pretty well-known fact that dancing—especially dirty dancing, the kind where you are virtually guaranteed to have close contact that often includes grinding and rubbing—often leads to sex. Hot, steamy sex! What are you waiting for? Hit the dance floor!

42 Try some porn, at least once.   Most people who claim not to like porn have never watched it. Or perhaps they just haven't watched the kind that suits their tastes. There are lots of different types of adult films out there: amateur/homemade, films made by—and for—women, soft porn, etc. Chances are, there is a category out there for you.

43 Explore oral.   Just as with porn, some people rule out oral sex without giving it a fair shot. Most of the common concerns or fears related to oral sex (such as being self-conscious about how you taste/smell) can easily be solved with simply strategies such as using flavored and/or scented body oil. Keep in mind: Many people find it much easier to experience orgasm via oral stimulation than through intercourse.

44 Give one sexual command.   If you can't bring yourself to give your partner step-by-step directions on how to please you sexually, start small by giving him one simple directive. Agree to let him do the same. The command can be something short and sweet, such as, "Let me be on top more often" or "Touch me there a little harder." 🖤🖤

45 **TRY A TOY.**   Now that you have ventured into porn pleasures, it is time to tiptoe your way into the world of toys. Sex toys, of course. If you're clueless (or just plain scared) when it comes to sex toys, they can seem intimidating. So start off small with, say, a sensual body feather or a simple blindfold. Tip: You can order plenty of toys online, from the safety and anonymity of your home. 🖤🖤🖤

46 **MAKE ONE CHANGE TO YOUR SEXUAL ROUTINE.**   News flash: It doesn't take much to shake things up in the bedroom, especially if you've fallen into a rut of doing the exact same stuff in the same sequence. It might be possible that your entire sex life could use an overhaul, but to keep things simple, start off small and make one change. It might be something that seems minor—say, having sex in the morning instead of at night. But when your sex life has gone stale, it doesn't take much to make things seem new and exciting again. 🖤🖤

47 **ANNOUNCE YOUR INTENTIONS WHILE YOU ARE BEING INTIMATE.**   This one is so simple, yet you won't believe how well it can work. Slowly and carefully announce each act before you do it. As in, "I'm going to lick your nipples until they're hard." Make your vocabulary as sweet or graphic as you and your

partner prefer. For added effect, wait a few beats after your announcement before doing anything. This teasing maneuver will have your partner squirming with anticipation.

48 **ASK PERMISSION.** Even if you already know what the answer will be, it is nice to ask, at least once in a while. This gesture works especially well with women. Ask permission before doing something, even if you know that you will definitely get the green light. For example: "May I enter you now?" or "May I kiss you there?"

49 **BE CONFIDENT (BUT NOT COCKY).** You may be self-conscious, but if you can fake it and act confident about your sexual prowess, your body, your techniques, or whatever, most likely your partner will be so charmed by your confidence he won't notice anything else. Think of Jamie Lee Curtis in *True Lies* when her mousy secretary character forced herself to do a striptease. After overcoming her nervousness, she put on a performance that could have fooled anyone.

50 **COME OUT OF THE DARKNESS.** Always do the deed in the dark? Shed some light on things. Conquer your inhibitions by adding light gradually: Start with candlelight, then add a little more light each night. This will be especially exciting for men, who tend to get aroused by visual stimulation and will love seeing their partner come out of the shadows.

51 HAVE A (VOLUNTARY) DRY SPELL. Even a long-time partner will seem new and exciting when you haven't seen each other—or at least, had a sexual encounter—for a while. Force yourself to go without sex for a while, and watch how your desire suddenly spikes.

52 HAVE A VOLUNTARY DRY SPELL—TWIST #1. Here is a new spin on the voluntary dry spell technique. You and your partner can engage in creative abstinence, in which only one particular act is off-limits, or where you can have foreplay but not the big payoff.

53 HAVE A VOLUNTARY DRY SPELL—TWIST #2. This is yet another variation of the voluntary dry spell. Spend a week getting each other hot via phone sex (or IM sex) without actually seeing each other at all during that period. It will make your reunion all that much more exciting.

54 AVOID THE SAME OLD THING. Make it a game to see how many of your tried-and-true moves and habits you and your partner can avoid for a specific period. Come up with a penalty to impose whenever you catch your partner falling back on one of the old standbys.

55 KISS WITH CREATIVITY. It's great to shake up your sexual routine, but the "variety can be cool" approach should start way before you get horizontal.

We're talking about kissing. Many couples don't do nearly as much as they should (we're talking real make-out sessions here, not hurried pecks on the cheek). And when they do kiss, it's usually like they're on auto-pilot. Try coming up with new and different kissing techniques. ♥♥♥

CHAPTER 2

PRE-ACTION MOOD ENHANCERS

If you want to really enjoy sex, you need to start thinking about it way before you actually hit the sheets. Preparation—and a little advance effort—can be the key to making sure things get hot in the bedroom. This is one time when forethought can really pay off big time. Put some thought and preparation into your sexual encounters, and you and your partner will reap the exciting rewards.

First, you've gotta get your motor running (not to mention, your partner's). Try these moves to help get you both in the mood. (Don't worry—they're simple!)

Things You Can Do for (or with) Your Partner

There are lots of things you can do for or with your partner that will help you both get into the proper mood for romance. Try a few of these strategies to maximize your chances of making some mad passionate love in the very near future.

56 PRACTICE SEXERCISE. Sex Squats. Dr. Cadell describes this sexy workout: "The squat exercise typically starts in a standing position. Feet should be approximately shoulder-width apart. You then bend at the knees until your thighs are parallel to the floor. Squat down above your lover's face (who is lying down comfortably while you do all the work) and let him or her touch or lick your genitals. Try to do five with two repetitions. Take turns doing the love squats if you can."

57 TRY SEXERCISE. Sexups. One person lies down on the floor face up while the other person lies on top face down toward the partner's feet (as in the sixty-nine position). With palms at shoulder level, legs apart on either side of the lover's head, the person on top pushes him- or herself up and then down so that both people are able to kiss each other's genitals. Try to do five with two repetitions. Take turns doing love push-ups.

58 TAKE YOGA TOGETHER. Yoga offers mental, spiritual, and physical benefits . . . not to mention, you will work up a sweat. With a multitude of compromising positions, yoga lets you see each other from many intriguing angles. Plus, it can lead to more vigorous exercise. Stretch your imagination . . . ♥

59 TRY TO FIND A YOGA CLASS DESIGNED ESPE-CIALLY FOR COUPLES. While taking a standard yoga class together is great, you'll enjoy some extra benefits by participating in a class designed specifically for couples. These classes often include techniques geared toward encouraging intimacy and strengthening your romantic bond. ♥

60 DO YOGA IN THE NUDE. When practicing yoga together at home, do it in the nude. Not only will the yoga poses allow you to appreciate your partner's body from many new and exciting viewpoints, but you will also be free of any restrictive clothing, which will enable more comfortable movements. ♥♥

61 READ SEX BOOKS TOGETHER. Read "how to please your lover" books (like this one!) to find new techniques for oral sex and other foreplay activities. You might be surprised at what you learn. Read the books aloud to your partner to make her crave and anticipate the events to come. ♥♥

62 WRITE A "LUST LIST." Make a list of ten things that drive you wild (in a good way) about your partner. You want it to be hot, so make sure the ten things are sexy and personal. Include things you love about your partner's body, the things he does in bed, how he makes you feel physically, etc.

63 LEAVE HIM A NAUGHTY REMINDER. Slip a pair of your panties, his favorites, into the pocket where he keeps his keys. They'll be the first thing he feels as he leaves the house, and you (and certain parts of your body) will be on his mind all day.

64 FLIRT WITH A STRANGER. No, we're not suggesting you pick up a stranger. We're talking innocent flirting here—the kind that isn't intended to lead anywhere else. Exchanging some harmless flirtations with an attractive stranger can boost your ego—and get you in a romantic mood when you meet up with your significant other. Be sure to do this only in safe situations, lest you find yourself with a new "admirer" you can't get rid of. Good options: an airport or train station when you are both going in different directions, so you're guaranteed not to see this person again.

65 FLIRT WITH A STRANGER—IN FRONT OF YOUR HONEY. This isn't for everyone. Your partner must be very secure in the relationship (and can't be the jealous type). But as long as you have no intention of taking it any further, this can be fun. For some people, seeing that their partner can grab attention from the opposite sex can be exciting. Plus, it just might make your partner realize what a good catch you are!

66 SHARE SOME SUGGESTIVE SENTIMENTS. To make your "little love notes" a bit spicier, add a suggestive picture of yourself—or a photo cut out of an adult magazine that illustrates what you'd like to do to your partner when she gets home. This will really give your partner a pick-me-up, and will make her eager to get home! 💗💗

67 SHARE SOME EXOTIC ENTERTAINMENT. Rent a juicy foreign film or two—the characters are often less sexually inhibited than in domestic films, and the plots are a little more "out there," and often punctuated with a little humor. It will give you something to talk about during and after sex! 💗💗

68 INVENT DIRTY CODE WORDS OR PHRASES TOGETHER. A secret language can help you communicate your love in the most unlikely of places—at a family lunch, or during a business meeting. Warning: It might be tough not to giggle when you and your partner are talking dirty in front of people who have no clue what naughty exchange they are missing. 💗

69 DOCUMENT YOUR (EROTIC) ARTWORK. Decorate your partner's body with edible body paints, and then take a tasteful picture of your handiwork for a souvenir of your time together. Take turns being the photographer and the model. Experiment with different types of paints. Eventually, you may even have enough pictures to fill an entire album. 💗💗

10 **MAKE SOME NEW SPECIAL (AND SEXY) OCCASIONS.** To put a sensual twist on your calendar, proclaim this your "year of sexy occasions." Vow to do something sexually exciting and/or daring on every special occasion, to create some sizzling memories. You will really start to look forward to those kids' birthday parties and neighborhood potlucks!

11 **KEEP THE FLAME ALIVE.** Save the wine bottle from a particularly special dinner you shared, and turn it into an oil lamp or candleholder. You can purchase a ceramic cork and wick from candle stores. Then, use this candle during special romantic interludes, to add a special nostalgic touch.

12 **SEND SOME EROTIC AIRMAIL.** Write something sexy on a piece of paper (or draw a naughty picture), and send it as a paper airplane over his shoulder to get him away from checking his e-mail or other chores. Once you have his attention, make the most of it.

13 **TREAT YOUR PARTNER TO A BATH, WITH A BONUS OR TWO.** Run a warm bath, and then make it extra special. Add some fragrant bath salts, bubble bath, or scented oils. If possible, warm up some towels so they will be cozy when the bath is finished.

14 **ENJOY A BATH FOR TWO.** Join your partner in a bath for two—but only if you're invited. Once in the tub, make the most of this special encounter. Help your partner get clean (or join her in getting "dirty"). Take advantage of the lubricating properties of warm, soapy water. 🖤🖤

Things You Can Do By Yourself (to Make Your Time Together Better)

Now that the two of you have spent lots of time doing romance-enhancing things together (or for each other), you may be ready for love. But there are other things that you can do individually that can also put you in the best possible frame of mind before you make sweet music together.

15 **STUDY THE BODY.** Take a class in which you learn about your partner's anatomy and how to please. Even if you already think you know your way around the human body pretty well, you will probably learn a few new things. You might even learn a few things about your own body as well. 🖤

16 **STUDY THE EROGENOUS ZONES.** Get a book (or do some research online) and find out about all of the erogenous zones on your partner's body. You probably already know about the obvious ones (as in, the genitals) but there are many others. You might be surprised to discover a few new ones! 🖤

Chapter 3

Setting the Scene

When it comes to keeping your sex life hot, never underestimate the importance of establishing the proper environment. By setting the right atmosphere, you give yourself (and your partner) a headstart for getting into a romantic mood. Making even some small changes to your love nest can really boost your urge to make some magic there. These tips can help you set the perfect stage for sensual encounters.

77 DO SOME HOUSEKEEPING—BUT MAKE IT SEXY. Nobody wants to get romantic in a room that looks like it's straight out of a frat house. Clean things up, and get rid of the clutter. This doesn't sound very exciting, right? Well, you can make the cleaning process itself a form of foreplay by doing it in the nude—or perhaps while wearing one of those sexy French maid outfits.

78 ESTABLISH A LOVERS' RETREAT. Surprise your partner by turning your bedroom into a boudoir. Drape scarves over that old chair and light some scented candles. Have some sexy finger foods such as strawberries and grapes, a bottle of your partner's favorite wine, and massage oils on the bedside table.

79 TRY TO FIND THE SMELL OF (SEXUAL) SUCCESS. You already know that scent can go a long way in establishing the right mood. Add candles or fragrant oils to your bedroom, and try a few different combinations until you find the one that you and your partner find most romantic.

80 BE WILLING TO TRY VARIETY WHEN IT COMES TO SCENTS. You've probably heard that different scents can affect your mood in different ways. Experiment with this theory. Alternate the scents in your romantic environment, trying a different one each night for a week. Note the results, and figure out which scents you do and don't find erotic.

81 **INSTALL A LOVE SWING IN YOUR BEDROOM.**
Dana Barish (*www.slumberpartiesbydana.com*) says a swing is
a perfect bedroom accessory—"It's easy to put up, and
easy to hide the evidence—a swing is sure to keep the
sex hot. You can get into sexual positions only thought
possible by gymnasts and yoga students."

82 **HANG A MIRROR ON YOUR CEILING.** Take a
page from the standard stud handbook. Sure, it's an
old cliché. But you just might like it. Many people,
especially men, find it a turn-on to watch themselves
having sex with their partners.

83 **MAKE LOVE ON A BED OF ROSES.** This is a
romantic classic that everyone should try at least once.
Spread a bunch of rose petals across your bed (and
around the floor). It may feel a bit unusual at first, but
it will smell great. It also makes for an ultraromantic
scene—and a great surprise for your lover!

84 **MAKE LOVE ON A BUNCH OF MONEY.** Spread a
bunch of money (one dollar bills would do fine) across
your bed. Have sex on top of it. Take turns scattering
some of the money across each other's bodies. This
really is not quite as sexy (or comfortable) as it appears
in the movies. But it is one of those things that everyone wants to be able to brag about doing.

85 **SET A SEXY TRAIL TO YOUR SEDUCTION SPOT.**
Set down a trail for your partner to follow. It should

lead right to your bed (or wherever you plan to seduce him). You can make a trail out of rose petals for a romantic touch. Candy kisses would also be a good choice. Of course, you could always go for a more blatant message—leave articles of your clothing as a trail, letting your partner know that you won't be wearing anything when he reaches the destination.

86 **SET THE STAGE FOR AN AMAZING INTIMATE ENCOUNTER.** Sure, props and costumes are great. (We will go into those in more detail later.) But for the total effect, go all out and set an entire scene. Depending on time/space constraints, you can really revamp your love nest to make it the prefect backdrop for whatever particular fantasy role-playing scene you may have in mind. Rearrange or remove furniture, add new elements—let your imagination run wild! Your partner will be shocked, and may wonder if he accidentally walked into the wrong house.

87 **CREATE YOUR OWN MAKE-BELIEVE CATHOUSE.** If you are pretending to be a "working girl," you can make your room look like what you'd envision a brothel to be—perhaps with satin pillows, dark colors, maybe even some gaudy décor. Of course, sex toys should always be nearby.

88 **BE A GOOD SPORT, IN THE RIGHT SETTING.** If you and your partner are enjoying a game of athlete and cheerleader, try to replicate a locker room or

maybe a gym (minus the stinky sweatsocks, of course). Bonus: Gym equipment can provide the perfect surface for some exciting sex play.

89 CREATE A HOT-AND-SEXY HOLDING CELL. If you and your partner like pretending to be a cop and a criminal as part of your role-playing activities, add some "law and order" touches to your space (hey, those handcuffs can always come in handy for lots of sexual activities, anyway).

90 MAKE YOUR OWN DEVIL'S PLAYGROUND. If one of you is planning to be really bad (or just wants to pretend to be really bad), or if you're going to be carrying out some S&M fantasies, you want to create a very dark atmosphere. Try rich colors, lots of velvet, and low lighting. Feel free to throw in some fake skulls or other gothic accessories, too.

91 TAKE SOLACE IN YOUR TANTRIC TEMPLE. Planning to engage in some Tantric sex? You want to establish a calm environment where you can become one with the universe and with each other. Turn your bedroom into a sacred sensual space with candles, scents, lots of pillows, and natural prints—plus, some décor related to the moon and stars wouldn't hurt.

92 ENJOY SOME ANIMAL MAGNETISM. If you plan to let loose your bare animal instincts and act like savages, you should go with a jungle theme when it comes to your bedroom décor. Try adding some animal-style accessories, like leopard and zebra prints, earth colors, and fur.

93 **USE SOME STRATEGIC CAMOUFLAGE TO MAKE YOUR PLACE SEXY.** Sure, it would be great to have your own love nest devoted just to sexual encounters. But this is the real world, and most likely you need to use that space for other stuff, too. To keep all your clutter and household necessities from spoiling the mood, be creative in covering things up. Use scarves or draperies to hide clutter, unsightly walls, or ugly windows.

CHAPTER 4

STEAMY SOLO MOVES

A couple is only as good (and good in bed) as the sum of its individual parts. Before you can both be sexy wild things together, you each need to be sexy—and comfortable with your sexuality—on your own. You can't show someone else how to operate the equipment if you have not yet learned how to work it yourself. In other words, you cannot expect your partner to please you until you have learned how to please yourself. Here are some sexy solo moves that will help you become a sexier half of a really hot couple.

94 SHAKE YOUR MONEYMAKER—FOR YOUR HONEY. Take a striptease class. It may take some time (and hard work) to master the moves, but it will be well worth it. Once you've perfected your routine, surprise him with your new moves.

95 PERFECT YOUR POLE SKILLS. Take it one step further and learn the art of pole dancing. Classes are available in many areas. Whether they want to admit it or not, few guys can resist the allure of a girl who knows how to work a pole. If you're really committed to the idea, you can even put a pole in your bedroom.

96 SUBMERSE YOURSELF INTO THE SHOWGIRL ROLE. Incorporate some role-playing. Wear a wig and talk with a sexy accent. Come up with a name for your stripper persona (like Candy or Savannah). Be sure to wear a garter belt, so your man can tip you generously (warn him beforehand to make sure he brings lots of singles). If the mood strikes, you can give him a special dance—or invite him back to the "VIP Lounge" for some extraspecial attention.

97 ADD A SHOWGIRL SOUNDTRACK. Once you have mastered your stripping and pole dancing routines, take it to the next level by putting together a complete show. Create a sexy routine to go with one of your partner's favorite songs (bonus points if it's the first song you ever made love to).

98 TOUCH YOURSELF. By now, everyone should know that masturbation is normal and healthy. Plus, it is usually our first "test lab" for discovering what we like (and don't like) sexually. Don't feel weird or embarrassed about exploring your own body. The more comfortable you are with yourself, the more comfortable you will be with a partner. ❤❤❤❤

99 WATCH (YOURSELF) AND LEARN HOW YOU LIKE TO BE PLEASURED. Masturbate in front of a mirror at least once or twice. Not only will it probably be enlightening and educational, but you might discover that it is a turn-on to see yourself reach a climax (without having to worry about anyone else watching you). ❤❤

100 GET A CLOSE-UP LOOK AT YOUR (EXCITED) INTIMATE PARTS. Masturbate using a small handheld mirror so that you can see a close-up view of exactly how your body responds. This might seem strange at first, but stick with it and really observe how your body reacts as you get more aroused. Most likely, you will learn lots of new and surprising things about your body and how it works. ❤❤

101 DO PC EXERCISES. Women: do your PC exercises (also known as Kegel exercises). This can help strengthen your pelvic muscles, which helps enhance the sexual experience. To perform these exercises, you simple squeeze your pelvic muscles as tightly as you can. (This is similar to what you would do if you were urinating and wanted to stop the flow.)

102 **BECOME A KEGEL QUEEN TO DEVELOP IMPRESSIVE SKILLS.** Keep practicing your Kegels often, gradually increasing the number of contractions you do in rapid succession. Eventually you may reach the point where you can pull off a trick favored by very talented strippers—picking up an object (something that can't cause injury—say a pillow or a dollar bill) by kneeling over it and contracting your vaginal muscles. Your partner will be amazed.

103 **SHARE THAT SEXY SQUEEZE AS A SPECIAL SURPRISE.** Without warning your partner, squeeze those PC muscles during intercourse. See if he notices. (If not, try it again, a bit more forcefully.) Most likely, the gripping sensation will thrill him. He will wonder where you learned this secret magical trick.

104 **FUCK A FAKE.** This is for the guys. Try a fake vagina. Think of it as a pretend pussy. There are lots of different types in all shapes and sizes. Some are even modeled after female porn stars' private parts. It's like the best of both worlds: you get the feeling of being with someone new, without the hassle or guilt of cheating.

105 **GET ORAL FROM A FAKE.** Guys: try a "mouth masturbation aid." This is a sex toy, with one end shaped like a mouth with open lips. It is usually made from a flexible rubberlike material, and is designed to provide a sucking motion when a penis (or anything else) is inserted into it.

106 **T**RY ARTIFICIAL ANAL. This is the latest version of the "fake body parts" line of sex toys for men. Like the others, it is usually made from a rubberlike material. It features an "anal opening" which is designed to give a nice tight fit (in a good way).

107 **P**LEASURE YOUR PROSTATE. The prostate has been called the "male g-spot" because it is rumored to have the potential for powerful pleasure, if stimulated the right way. To help with that goal, try the latest sex toy for men: a prostate stimulator. It straps on, to allow for hands-free pleasure. Obviously, this isn't for squeamish guys who do not like anything "back there" in that region at all.

CHAPTER 5

FANTASIES

Admit it—at some point in the recent past, you have fantasized about doing something sexually crazy and wild (even if you already consider yourself to be pretty crazy and wild). And no matter how satisfied you are with your sex life now, you have probably imagined what it would be like to be a totally different person in the bedroom. When it comes to spicing up your sex life, fantasyland is fertile ground. Fantasies are a popular—and reliable—way to make things more exciting. The best part? There are no limits, except the boundaries of your imagination. You can be as creative as you want. Dream up scenarios that are unlikely or even impossible in real life. Who cares if you couldn't or wouldn't really do this "in real life." That's the whole point! Indulging in a fantasy is like giving yourself permission to be as wild or crazy as you want. Unleash your inner wild child!

108 **SET SOME RULES BEFORE SHARING YOUR FANTASIES.** Before engaging in any fantasy-sharing (or role-playing) with a partner for the first time, establish ground rules. Here's an important one: Stress that just because you're excited by a certain scenario as a fantasy doesn't necessarily mean you want to engage in that scenario in real life. For example, many people enjoy fantasizing about a threesome, but wouldn't actually want to participate in one. On the other hand, sometimes (especially for shy types) fantasies can be a good way to broach the topic of something daring they might really like to try, but are embarrassed to suggest. Agree to use fantasies as a springboard to discuss things you may want to try, but with the understanding that there will be no pressure by either partner if one person prefers to leave that scenario strictly in fantasy-land territory.

109 **TRY THE NOTORIOUS THREESOME.** If you want to find one universal fantasy shared by both men and women, this is probably at the top of the list. It is especially popular among men, but more women fantasize about it than you might think (though many are too afraid to admit it). The exact gender combinations may vary (two men/one woman, or two women/one man) depending upon the individual. The level of participation you have in your fantasy vision may also vary greatly. Some people get turned on imagining themselves actively having sex with two other people, while others like the idea of being mainly a spectator while

their partner gets it on with someone else (or having their partner watch as they screw someone else). Your partner may get turned on if you share this fantasy with her, but there are two caveats. First, it is best to keep the third person in your fantasy threesome anonymous (at least in the version you share with your partner). Also, be warned that this may prompt your partner to try and coerce you to give the threesome scenario a whirl in real life.

110 WATCH TWO WOMEN TOGETHER. This is probably the most well-known of all sexual fantasies—at least, if you believe all the depictions on TV and in the movies, where men seem to turn to jelly at the mere thought of seeing two women kiss, let alone have sex. That may not be much of a stretch, as it does seem to be a very common fantasy among men. (Conversely, it is rare to hear a woman talk about wanting to see two men get it on.)

111 ENJOY A FANTASY FOURSOME (OR MORE). Group sex is another popular fantasy, although somewhat less common than the threesome scenario. Note: The funny thing about this fantasy (as opposed to the real-life actuality of group sex) is that, in the fantasy scenario, everything always goes perfectly. All of the participants are equally enthused and wind up equally satisfied. Not to mention, all the people involved are usually totally hot and very sexy. Oh, and nobody ever gets jealous or feels left out.

112 ¶MAGINE HAVING SEX WITH A CELEBRITY.
This is one fantasy that almost everyone has entertained. Admit it, ladies: You have fantasized about getting into bed (and waking up with) some hot actor or
rock star. And guys, I know you have imagined what
it would like to have some smoking hot actress on
her knees in front of you. In fact, this "sleeping with a
star" scenario is something people commonly envision
while pleasuring themselves. The bright side is that you
can usually safely share this fantasy with your partner,
unless they tend to suffer from very low self-esteem.
Few women are going to be worried that there is
much chance of you actually running off with, say, Pam
Anderson (at least, not unless you are a famous bad
boy rocker), so most likely it won't bother your partner
if you occasionally think about your celeb crush.

**113 ¶ANTASIZE ABOUT SEX WITH SOMEONE YOU
KNOW.** Fantasizing about someone you know can
be exciting (if you find him attractive) but can also be
unsettling. Trying to keep a straight face while talking
to your gardener—when just a few hours ago you had
imagined his head between your legs—can be tricky.
Warning: This fantasy is something you do not want to
share with your partner, unless he is supremely self-
confident and secure with your relationship. Even so, it
is probably still a bad idea.

**114 ¶ANTASIZE ABOUT SOMEONE YOU BOTH
THINK IS HOT.** Sharing a fantasy that involves a real

person you actually know can be risky, because it might cause your partner to feel insecure and wonder if you harbor a crush on (or worse, are having an affair with) this person. However, if there is a person or a couple whom you both find sexually attractive, you can engage in some joint fantasies about that person/couple.　♥

115 **IMAGINE SEX WITH SOMEONE YOU KNOW, BUT AREN'T ATTRACTED TO.** This can be disturbing—or at least annoying—for a different reason. If you don't like this person in real life, you may not be too happy about putting up with her in your fantasies. Again, avoid sharing this with your partner. She may try to read something into it, wondering if your supposed dislike of this person is really just a cover to mask your true lust for her.　♥

116 **FANTASIZE ABOUT SOMETHING YOUR PARTNER CAN'T/WON'T GIVE YOU.** Or at least, won't give you as often as you would like. For men, this often includes anal or oral sex. (Even if your partner does perform oral sex frequently, it may not seem like enough, especially if you are one of those guys who can never have enough.) In some cases, this fantasy may involve something your partner simply can't offer. For example, if your girlfriend is an A-cup but you fantasize about burying your face into some huge double-Ds, it is probably best not to mention this fantasy, since there is nothing your girlfriend can do about it (unless, of course, you are willing to pay for her boob job).　♥

117 FANTASIZE ABOUT MAKING SOMEONE BEG FOR IT. Everyone wants to be wanted. Even better is being wanted so badly that your admirer is willing to beg (or do anything else) in order to earn your affection and sexual attention. This is a popular fantasy among both men and women.

118 FANTASIZE ABOUT BEING A PROSTITUTE/ GIGOLO. In real life, selling your body for money usually comes out of desperation and necessity. It is rarely glamorous or exciting—and in fact is often a terrible nightmare. So why does it seem exciting as a fantasy? It's partly the *Pretty Woman* phenomenon. Many women who fantasize about prostitution (and, in fact, a good number of women who actually engage in prostitution) imagine themselves as Julia Roberts' hooker with a heart of gold, just waiting for a handsome millionaire to fall in love and sweep her off her feet and away from the street corner. For men, the idea of being a gigolo often seems exciting because it is like a form of flattery (all these women want me so much, they are willing to pay me to fuck them!).

119 FANTASIZE ABOUT PUTTING SOMEONE THROUGH PAIN OR HUMILIATION. In reality, you may be the sweetest person in the world—yet you find yourself fantasizing about spanking someone, making them do degrading things. What gives? This situation goes along with the "make them beg" fantasy—this person must want you really bad, if he is willing to endure all this. Plus, some people find it exciting to imagine the whole S&M aspect, even if they are not really interested in acting it out. ♥

120 FANTASIZE ABOUT BEING WITH A PROSTITUTE/ GIGOLO. People fantasize about being with a "pro" for the same reasons people claim to hire pros in real life: the chance to have wham-bam sex with no strings attached, from someone with "professional" skills (or, at the very least, someone who has presumably gotten pretty good at what she does). ♥♥

121 FANTASIZE ABOUT BEING A STRIPPER. It's usually women who fantasize about stripping. Again, the fantasy is a glamorized version of what is, in real life, often a depressing and unfulfilling role. Women who imagine being a stripper generally like the notion of having men lusting for them, and having control over these men (and their money). The woman who imagines being a stripper may also like the notion of being so comfortable with her body that she could show it off to strangers. For the shy girl, the notion of being an exhibitionist—and getting paid for it—can seem very exciting. ♥♥

122 FANTASIZE ABOUT SEX WITH A PARTNER NOT OF THE GENDER YOU USUALLY LIKE. So, for a straight woman, this would involve having sex with another woman. If you have never consciously entertained the thought of having sex with a partner of this gender, you might find this confusing. This fantasy can be especially unsettling for a straight man who finds himself imagining having sex with another man. But again, remember—this is just a fantasy, a pretend vision in your mind. It does not necessarily mean you have any real interest in engaging in that activity. Maybe your mind is just curious. Or maybe you ate something strange before going to sleep. Who knows? Bottom line: Don't waste too much time trying to overanalyze your fantasies. Just enjoy them.

123 **FANTASIZE ABOUT ANONYMOUS SEX.** Imagine having sex with a stranger whose name you don't know (and who, presumably, you would never see again). The cool thing about this scenario is that you can completely let your guard down and shed all your inhabitations. This fantasy partner has no expectations of you (except for immediate gratification) and will not be making any demands of you afterward. There are no strings attached and you don't need to worry about what he might think of you after you two have done the deed.

124 **FANTASIZE ABOUT SEX WITH SOMEONE WHOSE FACE YOU DON'T SEE.** In this scenario, you are having sex with someone without even seeing his face. That may be because he is wearing a mask or other clothing that obscures his face. Or perhaps it's because you're facing in the other direction. The advantage of this scenario is that you never need to make eye contact with the partner, or worry about how he might be looking at you. It is also helpful that you can either keep his identity unknown, or mentally substitute anyone you wish to be that stranger. ♥♥♥♥

125 **FANTASIZE ABOUT SEX IN THE DARK WITH UNSEEN PARTNER(S).** This is kind of a blend between the "sex with a stranger" fantasy and the "faceless partner" fantasy. In this scenario, you are somewhere that is totally dark so that you cannot see a thing (or, possibly, you are blindfolded). You then have sex with a partner—or perhaps several partners—without knowing anything about them. You might find yourself being serviced orally or manually without knowing the gender of the person who is pleasuring you. The nice thing about this fantasy is that it is your subconscious's way of freeing you of all hangups or preconceived notions you may have about potential partners. In your fantasy encounter, you know nothing about your partner(s). You do not know their gender, race, economic status, or nationality, and you know nothing about what they look like. Yet you discover they are able to satisfy you regardless of any of these characteristics. It can be a very freeing thought. ♥♥♥♥

126 **FANTASIZE ABOUT SEX THAT YOU DON'T WANT (OR SO YOU THINK).** This is a scenario in which you have sex with someone against your protests—usually these are initial protests, which you eventually give up on. In other words, you start out saying

"no" repeatedly—until eventually you say "yes." (That may quickly turn into, "Yes! Yes! Oh, yes!") The fantasy partner may be someone with whom you would not normally interact with, at least sexually. So this could be your mind's way of encouraging you to be a bit more open-minded. Another version of the "sex you don't want" fantasy involves your current partner springing a threesome on you unexpectedly. In this fantasy, your partner brings a third party into your bedroom (or wherever) and you initially resist, but later find yourself actively participating and enjoying it.

127 FANTASIZE ABOUT ANAL SEX. This fantasy is perhaps more common among men. But some women—especially those who rarely or never participate in anal sex in real life—may fantasize about it. This may be their way of trying to get more comfortable with the idea, and to perhaps work up the nerve to actually try it. Straight men who find themselves fantasizing about being on the receiving end of anal sex might find this disturbing.

128 FANTASIZE ABOUT BONDAGE/S&M. This fantasy can range from anything like spanking and blindfolds to the hardcore, such as chains, whips, and maybe even some painful options, like hot wax. You may want to fantasize about unleashing your inner dominatrix. Or perhaps your secret desire is to be on the other side of the coin—the sex slave. The nice thing about this fantasy: If you so wish, it's pretty easy to make it come true, at least to whatever extent you are comfortable with. Simply suggest to your partner that you try some light spanking, or maybe some slightly rough foreplay. ♥♥♥♥

129 FANTASIZE ABOUT DOMINATION. This fantasy may or may not also involve aspects of other fantasies (such as bondage/S&M). But your particular domination fantasy might simply involve being at the mercy of a dominating partner. This fantasy is especially common among people who tend to be submissive in their real sex lives. Perhaps it is a sign that you need to try exerting your dominant side once in a while. Your partner just might enjoy being the submissive one occasionally. ♥♥♥

130 FANTASIZE ABOUT SUBMISSION. On the other side of the coin, there is the submission fantasy. This is most often a fantasy of people who tend to be dominant in real life, and like to imagine what it would be like to be on the other side of the equation. This fantasy often occurs with men who are afraid to let down their dominant "persona" but secretly long to try out a more submissive role. ♥♥♥

131 FANTASIZE ABOUT WATCHING SOMEONE (WHOM YOU DO NOT KNOW) HAVE SEX. In this fantasy, you play the part of a voyeur, watching someone else's sexual escapades. Lots of people find this thought exciting, and it does not mean that deep down you have an urge to be a Peeping Tom. It is simply the concept of bringing porn to life—like watching an adult movie, only you are right there with the "actors." This fantasy often takes on an additional twist: either you pleasure yourself while watching (unbeknownst to the person/people you are watching), or you get caught, which may or may not turn out well.

132 **FANTASIZE ABOUT BEING WATCHED WHILE HAVING SEX WITH YOUR PARTNER.** In this fantasy, you get a thrill from being an exhibitionist. Most likely, the "audience" in your fantasy consists of strangers, but you may also find it exciting to fantasize about specific people you know watching you have sex. Some people bring this fantasy to life by making their own amateur porn tape, or by using a webcam to broadcast their sexual escapades online.

133 **FANTASIZE ABOUT HAVING YOUR PARTNER WATCH YOU HAVE SEX WITH SOMEONE ELSE.** Again, this fantasy often goes along with the idea of a threesome—but your partner is not actively participating in the action. In your fantasy, you may take things a step further, teasing your partner by allowing him to watch (especially if you are a woman, as is your fantasy partner) but not letting him join in.

134 **FANTASIZE ABOUT (SECRETLY) WATCHING YOUR PARTNER HAVE SEX WITH SOMEONE ELSE.** In this fantasy, you are hidden somewhere—

perhaps in a closet—and watch your partner having sex with someone else. In the more exciting version of this fantasy, your partner may be aware of your presence, but the other person is not. In that case, it is kind of a twist in the threesome fantasy—you are essential participating in a threesome as a spectator, but one of the parties is not aware of it. The more disturbing version of this fantasy involves you catching your partner cheating on you with someone else— but instead of confronting him, you keep watching while he is unaware of your presence. Naturally, you might try to read something into this fantasy. It might mean that deep down, you suspect your partner is unfaithful. But it may also simply mean that you find it exciting to imagine watching your partner with someone else.

135 **FANTASIZE ABOUT BEING NAKED, ON DISPLAY, FOR THE TAKING.** This is a fairly common fantasy among women (and some men). They imagine themselves naked and restrained, perhaps tied or chained somewhere (think: the woman in the early scenes of *King Kong*). They are helpless to stop any stranger from ravaging them, perhaps while others watch. This combines the erotic allure of several other fantasies (bondage, being watched, etc.) and puts them in one exciting package.

136 **FANTASIZE ABOUT BEING TAKEN AGAINST YOUR WILL.** This fantasy is perhaps the most controversial and unsettling (to the person experiencing it) of all fantasies. Understandably, many women are disturbed to find themselves imagining they are being taken by force, and may feel guilty about it (even if the fantasy occurs while they are dreaming and therefore have no control over what they imagine). Contrary to what these women may fear, this does not at all mean they actually want to be taken by force, or that they think rape would be fun. Remember, this is just pretend. It may simply mean you secretly wish your partner was a bit more forceful. Or that you think it would be exciting to have a dominating partner. Or it might mean nothing at all. The important thing is not to beat yourself up over a fantasy that might leave you puzzled or confused.

137 FANTASIZE ABOUT FORBIDDEN SEX. It is common to fantasize about sex with someone who is off-limits for whatever reason. This fantasy partner could be married, a teacher (with you as her student), dating your best friend—or maybe even a priest/nun. The allure here is obvious: We always want what we can't have.

138 FANTASIZE ABOUT BEING DEFLOWERED—IN SOME FANTASTIC WAY. If your first time wasn't straight out of a romance novel, it may have left you feeling a little disappointed. This is your chance to rewrite history. Fantasizing about losing your virginity in some amazing (or amazingly romantic) way can help you feel like you got a taste of what you may have missed out on. 🖤🖤🖤

139 **FANTASIZE ABOUT SEX IN AN EXCITING PLACE OR POSITION.** If you can't actually have sex in a particular location (say, out in the jungle), fantasizing about it is the next best thing. The same thing goes for fantasizing about a certain sex act or position that you can not (or will not) do in real life, for whatever reason. Hey, that's what your imagination is for—enjoy it! 🖤🖤🖤

140 **FANTASIZE ABOUT SEX WITH A FICTIONAL/ HISTORICAL FIGURE.** Maybe you have thought about Superman having his way with you in his frozen fortress. Or you might have imagined it would be sexy if you were Marc Antony ravaging the sexy Cleopatra. The key here is, those fantasy partners are unattainable, so this is one fantasy you can safely share with your real partner (although I can't promise she won't giggle a little bit). But she may just volunteer to do some sexy role-playing with you—being Mary Jane to your Spiderman. 🖤🖤

141 **FANTASIZE ABOUT SOMEONE ELSE—WHILE HAVING SEX WITH YOUR PARTNER.** This is very dangerous territory, so it's only for the very daring! But if a fleeting snippet of a fantasy like this pops into your head while you are getting busy with your partner, do everything in your power to chase this image from your brain immediately. For one thing, you run the risk of accidentally uttering your fantasy partner's name—which, needless to say, probably would not go over too well with the real-life partner having sex with you at that moment. If you find yourself regularly fantasizing about someone else while having sex with your partner—or, worse, if the only way you can have sex with your partner is to fantasize about someone else—it could be a sign of problems in your relationship.

CHAPTER 6

ROLE-PLAYING

Fantasies and role-playing go hand in hand. They both involve using your imagination to envision (and perhaps act out) what it would like to be a different person, or to be in a situation you probably couldn't or wouldn't actually do in real life. A fantasy generally involves just imagining a particular scenario. In role-playing, you take it a step further and act it out or pretend to be in that scenario. The line between fantasy and role-playing can be blurry. Whatever you call this type of erotic acting, many people consider it to be a sexual lifesaver. It can be especially helpful to couples who have been together for a while, and have fallen into a rut where their sex lives have gotten a bit stale. There are hundreds of fantasy and role-playing scenarios to choose from. Here are a bunch to get you started.

The Classics

When it comes to fantasy and role-playing scenarios, many have stood the test of time. Following are just some of the classics that have been helping people get their freak on for years. Not surprisingly, they have also been the premise for countless cheesy porn flicks. Take these staples of sex play and add some hot new twists to make them your own.

142 **BE A SEX SLAVE.** Dr. Cadell recommends this role-playing scenario. "You will need to clear your calendar for at least a full day so you may devote all of your time to satisfy the whims and desires of your lover. In fact, I would suggest making a weekend out of it— if you intend on being a good slave. The sex slave is someone who is available night or day, no questions asked. A great sex slave is someone who is willing to play the role wholeheartedly. Buy the perfect sex slave outfit to really get into the character. Leather and lace are good choices, but PVC (fake leather) is less expensive. Discuss your sexual boundaries before embarking on your slave and master role-playing so that you can respect each other's sexual limits. Then you must do whatever your lover tells you to do. Do as you are told. Don't forget to change roles on a separate occasion because it is a well-known fact that someone who has been a good slave can be a good master!"

143 **PRETEND TO BE AN ATHLETE AND CHEER-LEADER.** You may have never had a shot in hell of making it to the big leagues (or even the junior varsity

squad), but this is your chance to live out your dreams of being a "big baller." Maybe she can even create her own cheer especially for you. And if you have always thought cheerleaders were a bit snobby, here's your chance to put one in her place. The best part: You are virtually guaranteed to score!

144 **PRETEND TO BE A STEWARDESS AND PASSEN-GER.** Give new meaning to the term "cabin service." Having a stewardess at your service will make you feel like you are going first-class all the way, and you may find yourself in the "fully upright position" way before takeoff. If you can't join the Mile-High Club in real life, this can be a pretty exciting alternative.

145 **PRETEND TO BE A STEWARDESS AND CAP-TAIN.** Acting out this role-playing fantasy can take your sex life to new heights (pun intended). Be the master of your cockpit and show the sexy stewardess exactly what you mean by "captain's orders." To shake things up, the female partner could be the captain.

146 **PRETEND TO BE A NURSE AND PATIENT.** The best part about this scenario is, if you are the patient, all you have to do is lie in bed and enjoy the tender care of your knockout nurse. If you are really lucky, maybe she will even give you a sponge bath.

147 **PRETEND TO BE A NURSE AND DOCTOR.** Sneak off for a quickie in a supply closet, or give each

other an examination on an empty hospital bed. Use your imagination, and figure out lots of different ways to make "playing doctor" as hot as possible.

148 Act like an exhibitionist and voyeur. One of you gets to strut your stuff—naked, of course—while the other watches from some hidden vantage point. The exhibitionist can take advantage of the opportunity to put on a really enjoyable show for her secret admirer, perhaps even going out of her way to tease her Peeping Tom.

149 Pretend to be a boss and secretary. The "boss" can chase the "secretary" around the desk, or come up with some more creative types of sexual harassment. In a real office environment, it would be totally inappropriate to make your secretary service you orally from under the desk while you're on a conference call, or to make her answer your phone while she straddles you in the nude. Fortunately, this is your fantasy office, where anything goes.

150 Pretend you are a pool boy and rich lady. You are a strapping young man (probably late teens or early twenties), just trying to make a living in the hot sweaty sun—which forces you to take off your shirt, of course. Suddenly you spot the rich lady of the house, strutting around poolside in her skimpy bathing suit. She is older than you, but you can't help but notice how great she looks in that bikini. She asks you to get her a drink—and invites you to join her. Next she asks you to rub suntan lotion on her back. And a few other places . . .   ♥♥

151 PRETEND TO BE A REPAIRMAN AND LONELY HOUSEWIFE. Ah, the premise of many a classic porn flick. The virile young contractor arrives to fix the leaking roof—only to be greeted by the lonely housewife in her revealing negligee. She is bored and lonely at home by herself all day, and it has been way too long since she has been satisfied by a man. The repairman's job is to show her exactly what she's been missing—as long as he can finish the job before her husband gets home.   ♥♥♥

152 PRETEND TO BE A SAVAGE JUNGLE MAN AND CITY GIRL (THE "TARZAN AND JANE" STORYLINE). If you can manage to locate a loincloth, that would be perfect. If not, any kind of jungle-print bikini briefs will do. This is your man's chance to act totally uncivilized and follow his most basic raw instincts. The phrase "fucking like animals" is a perfect fit here. And if he wants to let loose with a "Tarzan yell" at the peak of excitement, all the better.   ♥♥♥

153 PRETEND YOU ARE A TEACHER AND STUDENT (THE TEACHER'S PET). In real life, of course, any sexual contact between these two would be a no-no. But in your fantasy world, there is no such taboo (well, maybe there is, but you are allowed to ignore it—that's what makes it so exciting). Let's see how far this student is willing to go in order to earn that A. She shouldn't be too shocked if her teacher bends her over the desk, entering her from behind (for added effect, the "student" could be sporting some cute pigtails that bounce up and down as the thrusting picks up speed).

154 **ROLE-PLAY AS A ROCK STAR AND GROUPIE.** You are the devoted female fan who would do anything—yes, anything—to get close to your favorite rock star. Even if you have to blow the entire road crew and flash your ass to every bodyguard backstage, you are determined to succeed in your mission. And it works—you finally make it onto the tour bus, where you can get up close and personal with the star himself. He offers to give you a tour of the bus, especially the bedroom, where you will have the chance to earn a VIP pass.

155 **PRETEND YOU ARE SWORN ENEMIES WHO CAN'T DENY THEIR SEXUAL ATTRACTION.** You (okay, your characters) aren't in love with each other. You don't even like each other, and most days can't stand to say more than a few words to each other. And yet there is an electric sexual energy between the two of you, and once you hit the sheets, you realize you have amazing physical chemistry. Can you put up with someone you can't stand in order to have mindblowing sex?

156 PRETEND TO BE A YOUNG INNOCENT MAN AND OLDER WOMAN. Think *The Graduate* (or, for younger folks, the video for "Stacy's Mom"). There's a reason that "cougars" are popular today. They have lots of tricks to teach a younger man—and get a thrill out of "breaking in" a wide-eyed innocent. For their part, the young men have stamina that older men may lack and they shower the woman with appreciation. And that tanned and toned body doesn't hurt.

157 PRETEND YOU (OR YOUR PARTNER) IS A FOREIGN STRANGER ON A TRAIN. You don't even need to speak the same language (in fact, it might make things easier if you didn't). This is one of those cases where actions speak louder than words. If your real-life partner actually has an accent—or can do a good job at faking one—that will make things all the more exciting. To really get the full effect, save this scenario for a time when you are actually taking a trip on a train.

158 PRETEND TO BE A BODYGUARD AND CELEBRITY. Make sure your man is clear about the fact that his duty is to guard your body, as closely as necessary. You are sick of hangers-on and star-fuckers just using you and bragging to their friends. You need a man you can trust with your safety and well-being—and any other personal needs you may have.

159 ROLE-PLAY AS A DOMINATRIX AND SLAVE. You get to decide which one of you plays each role—or you can take turns. Set some ground rules beforehand as to just how far you can go with the domination aspect and whether you can include humiliation techniques (some submissive types find it exciting to be humiliated—say, being called nasty names or being forced to do menial labor). If you really want to dive into the deep end of domination, break out some whips, chains, or other accessories.

160 ROLE-PLAY AS A GOOD GIRL AND BAD BOY. This is a classic "opposites attract" pairing. It usually ends up with the bad boy corrupting the good girl—or the girl shedding her Miss Goody Two Shoes skin. Think Olivia Newton-John and John Travolta in *Grease*. Or, you could turn it around, and make the good girl the seducer (think Molly Ringwald pouncing on Judd Nelson in the closet in *The Breakfast Club*).

161 PRETEND YOU ARE A COWBOY AND CITY GIRL. One thing cowboys know is how to get dirty. They also tend to know a lot about mounting and riding. City girls don't know much about rodeos, but they do know how to look sexy in high heels. They also really appreciate how great a man's ass can look in a pair of tight, well-worn jeans.

162 PRETEND YOU ARE A COWBOY AND NATIVE AMERICAN PRINCESS. The two of you have a forbidden love, posing danger to both of you if you are caught. But your burning passion will not be denied. He loves your long, dark braids and exotic face painting. Maybe you should give him a tour of your tepee. 🔥🔥

163 **ROLE-PLAY AS A LIBRARIAN AND FRAT BOY WHO LOOSENS HER UP.** You are the mousy, uptight librarian badly in need of a man who can loosen that bun of yours and help you let your hair down. He's a laid-back frat boy, always ready for a good time. The only question is: Will you get busy in the frat house or in one of the cramped aisles of the library's reference section? 🔥🔥

164 **PRETEND TO BE A COP AND CRIMINAL.** You can start things off with a thorough frisking, but most likely a strip search will be necessary at some point. And this is the perfect time to break out those hand-cuffs! For the woman playing the role of the criminal, you know what to do (hint: think Sharon Stone in *Basic Instinct*). 🔥🔥🔥🔥

165 **PRETEND YOU ARE A SECRET OPERATIVE AND FOREIGN SPY.** Think James Bond and any of his sexy female sparring partners. Or Jack Bauer and a female terror suspect (okay, Jack may not be foreign, but most women would say he is pretty sexy). They have ways of making you talk—and doing anything else they might desire. 🔥🔥🔥🔥

166 PRETEND YOU ARE A PRISON GUARD AND FEMALE INMATE. A girl can get awfully lonely, going without the company of a man for so long. See if you can earn some privileges for "good behavior." You can help get your guard in the mood by sharing highlights from all the lesbian sex you've been having with the other inmates. Guard: Don't forget the body cavity search.

167 PRETEND TO BE A PROSTITUTE AND CLIENT. You and your partner can pretend to be Julia Roberts and Richard Gere—or a much dirtier, raunchier pair of temporary lovers. The ending of this story is totally up to you to decide . . . as is your "asking price."

168 PRETEND TO BE A GIGOLO AND CLIENT. Now, switch roles and add a new spin. This time, the woman is paying—she is not easy to please, and she wants to get her money's worth. The more satisfied she is, the more generous she will be when giving her hired lover his tip.

Some New Twists

Now that you have gotten familiar with many of the old faithful role-playing scenarios, let's try a few new ones. These are sexy new spins on old standbys.

169 ROLE-PLAY AS CELEBRITY AND PAPARAZZO. This is a modern and timely premise, with celebs and their photog stalkers making the news so often these days. Unlike the old days of Hollywood when the press kept a respectable distance, modern photographers like to get up close and personal (sometimes really personal) with their famous prey. One of you pretends to be the star, while the other is a relentless photographer who will stop at nothing to get the unbelievable shot. The photog gets some intimate shots of the star—maybe even some very revealing shots—when the celeb finally decides to try and turn on the charm in order to win over the photographer. Once the celeb has successfully seduced the horny shutterbug, she shows him a real "money shot."

170 **PRETEND TO BE A POWERFUL LEADER AND INTERN.** You can probably guess what notorious encounter inspired this one. Service your partner while he is on the phone, seated at a desk. Throw in the cigar-related move, too, if you like.

171 **ROLE-PLAY AS A DOCTOR AND PATIENT.** The person playing the doctor role must maintain a serious and "professional" demeanor for as long as possible. They must use clinical words for body parts, address the "patient" by their formal name ("Miss Jones" or "Mr. Smith") and refute any "inappropriate" advances by their pretend patient. This will either totally turn you on, or cause you to break out into laughter.

172 **ROLE-PLAY AS A FEMALE BOSS AND MALE ASSISTANT.** In the traditional scenario, the man usually plays the role of the boss and the woman is his assistant. The modern spin is that the woman is now the (horny and demanding) boss, and the male partner is her eager-to-please assistant.

173 ROLE-PLAY AS A FEMALE ROCK STAR. Generally, in the rock star fantasy, the male assumes the role of the rock star. Why should guys have all the fun? This time, the female partner gets to be the rock star (try picturing Madonna or Christina Aguilera for inspiration), and the male partner is the groupie.

174 PRETEND TO BE A FEMALE SECURITY GUARD AND MALE GROUPIE. First, the female partner pretends to be the security guard who is blocking access to the backstage area. The male partner is the groupie who must come up with a creative way to please her in order to be granted a backstage pass.

175 PRETEND TO BE A ROADIE. Instead of a groupie, in this version, the male partner is now a roadie who lugs the female star's equipment around. Seeing the hot guy all flexed and sweaty, the rock star decides to assign him to a different role in her "crew."

176 TRADE PLACES. This is the simplest way to role-play—but it can also be very exciting, and may open your eyes to a whole new approach when it comes to sex. You simply flip your usual roles, with you assuming the normal strategies of your partner and vice versa. Some examples follow. 🖤🖤

177 **ASSUME AN INITIATOR ROLE FOR A CHANGE.** If you are rarely the one who initiates sex, what are you waiting for? Summon up your courage and just go for it. Your partner will probably welcome this new side of you—and will enjoy having a night off from the initiator role. 🖤🖤

178 **ADD A SEXY INCENTIVE CAN HELP WITH YOUR INITIATOR ROLE.** To help nudge you along, establish a rule whereby you two will not have sex for a week except for when you initiate it. After a few frustrating sexless nights, you will quickly overcome any qualms or fears you may have. 🖤

179 **SWITCH AROUND THE SUBMISSIVE ROLE.** If you are usually the submissive one, this is your chance to unleash your inner dominatrix. Be as bossy and domineering as you like! You might be surprised at how much you enjoy being in charge. And your partner may find that he likes playing the submissive role. 🖤🖤

180 **BECOME A VOCAL VIXEN.** Are you usually quiet as a mouse in bed? Time to kiss your Silent Sally persona goodbye. Make some noise! Scream, yell, moan—anything, just be vocal. Make it blatantly obvious that you are having a hell of a good time. 🖤🖤

181 KEEP YOUR PARTNER QUIET. If your partner is usually the more vocal, your job is to make him or her be quiet. See how much he can restrain himself before he can no longer resist yelling or moaning. If you like, you can tease him a bit by deliberately trying to make it tough for him to stay quiet.

182 ROLE-PLAY TOGETHER IN PUBLIC. Adopt a new persona together as a couple. If you are both usually more reserved and private, try engaging in some public displays of affection. Or, act like you are a pair of uninhibited exhibitionists. Take it as far as you dare.

183 PRETEND TO BE STRANGERS. Arrive separately at a restaurant or bar. Act like you've spotted each other from across the room, or pretend one of you is trying to pick up the other one. Even if nobody else pays attention, it will feel risqué to the two of you. Some twists on this scenario follow.

184 GET INTO A FAKE FIGHT. (Or, perhaps, take advantage of the opportunity to air pent-up differences and give yourself permission to engage in a real one.) Make a scene if you like. Then immediately engage in some hot "I'm so mad I'm turned on" sex. And perhaps follow that up with some make-up sex.

185 TAKE YOUR TIME JOINING UP WITH EACH OTHER. While acting out this scenario, prolong the excitement by taking your time reuniting. Perhaps stop along the way to chat—or even flirt—with members of the opposite sex. It will heighten the anticipation and make you want each other even more.

186 DO AN EROTIC FAKE INTERVIEW. Pretend you are a reporter for an adult magazine, and interview your partner about their sex habits and turn-ons—in public where someone might overhear you.

187 BE A DOMINANT MALE IN THE AGE OF FEMINISM. The next time you go to a fancy restaurant, order for her—such as, "The lady will have the shrimp cocktail, house salad with French dressing, and the coq au vin." Then order yours and the wine. It will make you seem very James Bond, and you can carry that all the way to the bedroom.

188 PUT ON A SHOW WITH YOUR "PRETEND STRANGERS" ACT. For the ladies: get a wig, sunglasses, and sexy clothes in a style that you wouldn't likely wear. Plan on bumping into your husband at some point during the day, and ask him out on a date after work. Have him meet you in the bar at a restaurant you don't usually frequent, and have fun with your new persona—show a little cleavage, rub up against him, act like a tramp, and draw attention from the other patrons. It'll be a turn-on for both of you.

189 BE A DOMINATRIX WHO DOESN'T ALLOW TOUCHING. Many dominatrixes claim they don't actually have sex with their clients. Try that out. Order your sex slave around (their "chores" can be sexual or nonsexual, or a combination of both). See what ideas you can come up with that are enjoyable for both of you, yet may not involve the two of you actually having sex. Perhaps the dominatrix can simply dictate the slave's masturbation technique/process.

190 COPY THE HOT (AND HORNY) COUPLE. We all know a person or couple who, we're sure, has the most amazing sex life. Often we know this because they go out of their way to tell us all about it. Surely, you have envied their wild exploits, so now is your chance to imagine exactly what they're doing behind closed doors. Pretend you're this person/couple, and act out some of their wild exploits. They're not shy or timid, so you don't need to be either. Feel free to act as carefree and uninhibited as you like.

191 FIND OUT IF BLOWHARDS GET BLOWJOBS. Another twist: Think of a person you find really annoying—perhaps a blowhard or someone who is really arrogant. Imagine what you think he'd be like in the bedroom, and act that out. This may not necessarily be steamy, but will probably be hilarious. For example, the blowhard may be so uptight that he nearly has a heart attack when his female partner tries something kinky. And the egomaniac may be so hypnotized by his own reflection in the mirror that he totally ignores his partner.

192 **G**ET SEXY WITH THE SOAPS AS YOUR INSPIRATION. Act out steamy scenes from your favorite soap opera or sexy show. Better yet, spend a week in which you must recreate a scene every day from your favorite episodes. Bonus: Ladies, this is one time when your guy won't complain about you watching soap operas. 🖤🖤

193 **D**O SOME EROTIC ACTING. Agree that you and your partner can each pick three scenes from any show/movie (you can include adult movies, if you wish) that you will then act out together. This gives you a way to act out fantasies that you may be too embarrassed to suggest otherwise. 🖤🖤

194 **I**MITATE A ONE-NIGHT STAND. One-night stands can have their allure. If you have been with your partner for a while, you may occasionally think back to those days of casual hookups. And if you have never had a one-night stand, you may wonder what you're missing. This is your chance to find out. Pretend one of you has picked up the other one in a bar. You will never see each other again, so you don't care what the other person thinks of you. All you care about is immediate sexual gratification. 🖤🖤

195 **A**CT OUT THE ROLES OF PAINTER AND MODEL. Pretend one of you is a world-renowned artist, and the other partner is her model (her nude model, perhaps). The partner in the model role must do whatever is asked of him . . . purely for the sake of art, of course.

196 ACT OUT THE ROLES OF A STRIPPER AND HER CLIENT. She is the sexy stripper who puts on a good show and has her male admirer drooling over all her. The male partner is the eager customer who is willing to fork over all the cash in his wallet for a lap dance.

197 ACT OUT THE ROLES OF A MALE STRIPPER AND HIS CLIENT. Switch things around. Now it's the man's turn to strut his stuff in order to turn on his female admirer. If she likes what she sees, she can reward him with a few dollars tucked into strategic places.

198 ACT OUT THE ROLES OF AN EAGER STUDENT AND HIS OR HER IMPROPER PROFESSOR. The student is willing to do anything to earn that good grade. To really make things interesting, pretend you are taking a class in anatomy or sex ed. Come up with some creative ways to earn extra credit.

199 ACT OUT THE ROLES OF A NERVOUS VIRGIN AND "THEIR FIRST." In this scenario, one of you is the innocent virgin, and the other is the much more experienced, savvy sex expert. You can decide whether the virgin is truly nervous and reluctant, or just pretending to be.

200 ACT OUT THE ROLES OF A PAIR OF VIRGINS. To make the virgin scenario more interesting, pretend you are both virgins. Share your wonder at discovering all these new experiences and feelings—and stumble your way around, trying to figure out how everything works.

201 ACT OUT THE ROLES OF A MECHANIC AND FEMALE CUSTOMER. She is an uptown woman willing to pay whatever it takes to get serviced. And she kind of likes getting dirty with a blue-collar guy. Perhaps a thorough lube job might be in order?

202 ACT OUT THE ROLES OF A LOWLY MALE EMPLOYEE AND THE BOSS'S DAUGHTER. You work in the mailroom, she is the boss's beautiful daughter. She wants you to be her boy toy, and you will do whatever it takes to keep her happy so she doesn't tell Daddy.

203 ACT OUT THE ROLES OF STAR-CROSSED LOVERS. She is from the east side, you're from the west. Or she's a Jet, you're a Shark. (Or perhaps a Democrat and a Republican.) Bottom line, you shouldn't be together. You can't be together. But you can't deny your passion, so you sneak off for dangerous liaisons.

204 ACT OUT THE ROLE OF AN UPTOWN WIFE AND THE SEXY TENNIS PRO. She is rich, spoiled, and easy on the eyes. And since her husband is always away on business, she is in need of attention. You are tan, fit, and blond. Show her a thing or two about balls and strokes.

205 ACT OUT THE ROLES OF A LIFEGUARD AND THE BUSTY BIKINI BABE. You are both hot, tan, and wearing skimpy clothes. Oh, and you are probably soaking wet, or slathered in suntan oil. You will need to rescue her, and some mouth-to-mouth just might be necessary.

206 PRETEND YOU ARE AN UPTIGHT BUSINESS-MAN AND A STREET-SMART GIRL. You wear a suit and tie. She wears leather. You could never take her home to Mom, but you sure would like to take her—right here and now. She can help you loosen up, and you can show her what's underneath that dress shirt of yours.

207 ACT OUT THE ROLES OF A GANGSTER AND HIS MOB MOLL. He is dangerous, unpredictable, and bends to nobody. Except, of course, when he bends over for you, behind closed doors. What would his "soldiers" think if they knew how much their macho boss enjoys being spanked?

208 ACT OUT THE ROLES OF A HOSTAGE AND CAPTOR. You have been taken prisoner, and your partner is assigned to be your guard. He must do his duty, but this is tough for him because he thinks you're cute. See if you can somehow earn a few favors from him.

209 PRETEND YOU ARE A PAIR OF SAME-SEX LOVERS. This might not be for everyone, but if you are up for it, pretend being two lesbians or two homosexual men. Use this opportunity to try out some new sex toys—or use your old ones in new and different ways.

210 ACT OUT THE ROLES OF SEXY LAWYER AND DESPERATE CLIENT. You are a hardened (or just plain hard) criminal and she is your buttoned-up attorney. You may be as guilty as sin, but you still want her to get you off . . . as many times as possible.

211 TAME THE SHREW. Inspired by the movie, this role-play is where the female partner is a wild woman who can't be tamed—until she meets the one man with the guts to put her in her place (while having hot steamy sex).

212 BE THE VOYEUR. Dr. Cadell suggests, "Use a telescope to spy on your lover. As long as you are both aware of the game being played, there's certainly no harm in watching your lover get undressed. If it's possible, set up your telescope in a building directly across the way (for the best possible view). If that's out of the question, at least set up shop outside your house, perhaps behind a tree that will not attract any attention from your neighbors (but it will still give you a clear view). Knowing that the other is watching will add an element of drama to this game of peekaboo." ♥♥♥

CHAPTER 7

FOREPLAY

When it comes to spicing up your sex life, foreplay is fundamental. Unfortunately, many couples underestimate the importance of foreplay. Often, long-term couples make the mistake of thinking they can skip it (been there, done that). In reality, more foreplay—and more exciting foreplay—might be just what bored lovers need to bring back their bedroom sparks. So, consider this an order: Focus on the foreplay (and enjoy the results).

213 ENGAGE IN SOME HEAVY PETTING...whatever your definition of that is. Perhaps you will just feel each other up, or maybe you will try some dry humping. Sure, now that you're adults, you can go all the way. But sometimes it's fun just to get a little taste.

214 ACT LIKE (HORNY YET HESITANT) KIDS AGAIN. Pretend you are teenagers again, and imagine that you are each just hoping to get to first (or maybe second) base. You may have reached the point where you take it for granted, but sometimes just getting that far can be a big thrill.

215 PRETEND YOU'RE AFRAID TO GET CAUGHT. Start with the premise of being horny teenagers just trying to get what you can. Now add an extra twist: Pretend the two of you need to be as sneaky (and quiet) as possible so your parents don't catch you.

216 GIVE HIM A HAND. On the list of sexual activities, handjobs often get overlooked. Yet they can be surprisingly effective. If you don't have time for intercourse (or simply don't want to "go all the way" for whatever reason), this is a good way to satisfy your man. Try different strokes and techniques to see which he prefers—then alternate between a few speeds/movements to keep things exciting.

217 GIVE HIM A HAND—AND YOUR MOUTH. Sure, fellatio is terrific all on its own. But to give your guy even more of a thrill, add some hand action. Stroke his shaft while going down on him—and don't forget to caress his testicles while you're at it. If he allows, you can also use your hand to stimulate his "secret spot" or his anal area while performing fellatio.

218 LEAVE THEM READY—AND WAITING. This is a good way to really tease your partner. Get him all warmed up and ready for action. If possible, put him in restraints or lock the bedroom door. The point is to leave him pretty much stuck in place. Tell him you need to get something and leave him there for a while. Wait for him to squirm a bit and really get all hot and bothered.

219 LEAVE HIM READY AND WAITING... and listening to you having fun. Leave your partner hot and bothered and unable to move. Then go into another room within hearing distance. Tell him that he has been a bad boy so you have decided to start without him. Moan and make other sounds like you are getting aroused. (You can either actually pleasure yourself, or just fake it.) He will be begging for your return.

220 LEAVE HIM HOT AND BOTHERED—AND REALLY TEMPTED. Leave your excited partner in the room, restrained—but this time leave an adult movie playing where your partner can see it. (Make sure his hands are secured away from his body to prevent him from trying to pleasure himself.) This will be sweet torture—and he will be ready to ravage you when you finally return and end the wait.   🖤🖤🖤🖤

221 ENGAGE IN SOME "KISSING QUICKIES." Enjoying a really good makeout session can get you in the mood for more, but can also be thrilling on its own. To heighten the excitement, throw in the attraction of a quickie. Sneak in a makeout session when you have a built-in time limit or have a chance of being interrupted—say, while at a red light in your car, or while one of you is waiting for the carpool to arrive. Knowing you might run out of time will be sure to add an extra thrill—and motivate you to make the most of your time.   🖤🖤

222 FELLATE YOUR PARTNER'S THUMB DURING FOREPLAY. This is a suggestion by Mark Michaels and Patricia Johnson, authors of *Tantra for Erotic Empowerment*. They say this trick will send a tingle to another part of your partner's body.   🖤

223 POLISH THE PEARL. That's the Tantric expression for performing oral sex on a woman. Almost all guys love receiving oral sex, but they should also be willing to return the favor. If you don't go down on your woman (or don't do it as often as you should), get down on your knees . . . and beg for her forgiveness. And then get to work while you're down there. If your woman is reluctant to be on the receiving end of oral (and some are, especially if they have never tried it), try to ease her fears. If she is worried about the way she smells or tastes, try using flavored lotions or treating her to a sensual bath beforehand.

224 **BE CREATIVE WITH HOUSEHOLD ITEMS.** A tip from Dr. Cadell: "There are lots of common household items you can use for creative foreplay, including a feather duster for tickling, a rolling pin for massaging, and a spatula for spanking, just to name a few. See how many common household items you can find to incorporate into foreplay. Don't forget to use your closet by convincing your lover that helping to tidy up the closet can be a sensual thrill."

225 **COVER YOUR PARTNER'S EARS WHEN HE OR SHE GOES DOWN ON YOU.** Michaels and Johnson say the sensory deprivation will relax and excite him or her.

226 **LET HIM THRUST BETWEEN YOUR BREASTS.** Most men love to do this. Squeeze your breasts together, with his penis in between them, and let him thrust back and forth. This is sometimes called "tit fucking" and men love watching themselves do it.

227 **LET HIM COME BETWEEN YOUR BREASTS.** Chances are, once he gets his penis anywhere near your breasts, he will get himself so worked up that this is what he will really want to do. Not to mention, the sight of it will be a big turn-on.

228 **GENTLY RUB HER BREASTS.** In their eagerness to fondle a woman's breasts, some men get a bit too rough and just manhandle them. Start out gingerly, and touch them gently. Most women like their breasts to be caressed softly. A tickling or flicking motion across the nipples can also feel good. If she indicates that she likes it a bit rougher, proceed gradually, stopping at the first sign of discomfort on her part. Never twist the breasts like a radio dial—most women don't like that, and it can be painful.

229 **LADIES, RUB YOUR OWN BREASTS.** It's so simple, yet very pleasurable for a man to watch. Caress your own breasts, and perhaps flick your nipples to help get them hard. Let him know how much you are enjoying your own body. He will be aroused in no time.

230 **LICK HER BREASTS, BUT DO IT GENTLY (AT LEAST AT FIRST).** You need to start out slowly and proceed carefully, gauging your partner's preferences. Some women enjoy it when you suck their breasts, while others find that unpleasant or uncomfortable and can only tolerate quick tongue-flicking.

231 **LADIES, TRY TO LICK YOUR OWN BREASTS.** Or at the very least, do your best to make a good show of it. This is an old stripper trick, and it usually drives guys wild. It might take a little bit of practice, but most women can eventually master this move.

232 **L**ADIES, LICK CHOCOLATE OFF YOUR OWN BREASTS. Again, the sight of this will really turn him on. Use any edible substance. And the taste will probably make this version of the breast-licking move a bit more appealing to you. If you are feeling really generous, you might allow your partner to take a lick or two as well.

233 **C**OMPLIMENT HER BREASTS. Many women are self-conscious about the size or shape of their breasts. Be sure to let your partner know how much you love them and how beautiful you think they are. Of course, actions speak louder than words, so if you seem very eager to see, touch, or fondle her breasts, that will let her know just how much you really like them.

234 **T**EASE HIS NIPPLES. Men love women's breasts, and usually incorporate them into foreplay. When it comes to their own breasts, however, guys are much more wishy-washy. Physically, the male breasts are just as sensitive as women's. So the potential for enjoyment by physical contact is definitely there. However, many men are uncomfortable with any kind of contact or attention focused on their breasts. Test your guy's comfort level by lightly flicking your tongue across or near his nipples. You can also use a scarf or feather to tickle this area. If he seems receptive, continue. If not, don't push it.

235 **NIBBLE ON THE TIP OF YOUR PARTNER'S NOSE.** Patricia Johnson says, "Much as a kiss can send chills throughout the body, licking and nibbling the tip of the nose can produce the same effect." ♥

236 **LICK YOUR PARTNER'S NECK.** If done correctly, this move is often well received by both men and women. Do it gently, with a light touch. Tease your partner with quick flicks of your tongue. Also, try to avoid too much moisture, or your partner will feel like she has just been drooled on. ♥

237 **BITE YOUR PARTNER'S NECK.** This is a soft and gentle nibble—don't do anything remotely resembling Dracula's techniques, as that will not go over too well with your partner. Any neck-biting moves that could possibly draw blood are (generally) not a turn-on. ♥

238 **GIVE YOUR PARTNER A HICKEY.** Yes, these "love marks" are usually just for teenagers, but the feeling can be enjoyable (as long as you don't suck too hard). You should ask permission first, or make sure the hickey is in a place that isn't easily visible. He might not be too thrilled about hearing the jeers and comments from his coworkers if they spot a gigantic purple hickey on his neck. ♥

239 **GIVE YOUR PARTNER A HICKEY—IN A VERY PRIVATE PLACE . . .** say, on the upper thigh. Nobody else will know it's there, so it's like your own little secret. And in order to get it there, you will need to do some sucking, which your partner will definitely enjoy. ♥♥♥

240 **LICK YOUR PARTNER'S EAR.** Again, gentle and soft are the key techniques here. Concentrate on the lobe and the outer part of the ear. Trying to ram your tongue directly inside your partner's ear will not feel pleasant—and could possibly result in some serious inner ear damage. ♥

241 **NIBBLE ON YOUR PARTNER'S EAR.** Just as with the neck-biting approach, the key is not to bite too hard. A soft nibble can feel good; a forceful bite does not. Plus, it might leave a scar. When putting your mouth anywhere near an ear, be sure to check for earrings first, so as not to accidentally bite down on one. ♥

242 **BLOW IN YOUR PARTNER'S EAR, GENTLY.** This is an old trick, and was featured on an episode (or several) of *Happy Days*. Make sure to blow very softly—forcing too much air into anyone's ear is dangerous, and suffering a ruptured eardrum is definitely not sexy. ♥

243 **CARESS YOUR PARTNER'S HAND.** A tip from Michaels and Johnson: Try placing the palm of your partner's hand over your mouth and kissing it deeply—when you're both really turned on. The stimulation will send shivers up the receiver's arm and throughout the whole body. ♥

244 **LICK YOUR PARTNER'S ANAL OPENING.** Not everyone would want to do this (or be on the receiving end of it, for that matter), but you might want to give it a try. You don't need to plunge your tongue all the way in there—some light tickling around the edges would be fine.

245 **LICK, SNORT, OR EAT SOMETHING OFF OF YOUR PARTNER'S ASS.** Think of the scene with Jack Nicholson and the cocaine-coated hooker in *The Departed*. This move is something everyone wants to do (guys, anyway) just because it looks hot—and bad. Just be sure to avoid anything sharp, hot, or spicy.

246 **STIMULATE THE SACRAL NERVES.** You can stimulate these nerves (located at the small of the back) with pressure, percussion, or vibration—pressing your hand firmly, moving it back and forth in short rapid motions, or tapping gently with the edges of your hands. Mark Michaels, author of *Tantra for Erotic Empowerment*, says, "The sacral nerves connect to the genitals, so you'll be sending a direct signal."

247 **GIVE YOUR PARTNER A MASSAGE.** It does not necessarily need to be particularly sensual. A basic massage helps relax the muscles and rid the body of stress. A relaxed, stress-free body is one that is more agreeable to romance and intimacy. Plus, your partner will be appreciative of this gesture.

248 GIVE YOUR PARTNER A SENSUAL MASSAGE.
A basic massage is good, but now try stepping it up a bit to make things sexier. Add some warming oil, scented lotion, or other sensual touches. Pay attention to the entire body, making sure to cover all of the erogenous zones as well as some "off the beaten track" parts that tend to get neglected. Encourage your partner to do some deep breathing. Then try to match your breathing to theirs. This "breathing in sync" technique helps promote intimacy and gets your bodies in a matching rhythm.

249 GIVE YOUR MAN A "MASCULINE MASSAGE."
This is a massage that focuses on his manly parts. Have him lie on his back with a pillow under his head and neck for comfort. Place another pillow under his hips to allow you better access, and to give him a better view of the action. Use some massage oil or warming gel, and start out slowly. Take your time, giving attention to all parts of his intimate area: the shaft, testicles, and even up to the pubic bone.

250 MASSAGE HIS REAR AREAS. Have him turn on his stomach and pay attention to his forgotten side. Start with the upper thighs or lower back and work your way to the buttocks. These muscles can get sore, especially after a long day at work, so it can be helpful to knead the buttocks to help work out the kinks and release stress in that area. Carefully (and tentatively) approach the anal area, probing a little at a time as you judge his comfort level with contact.　♥♥♥

251 GIVE YOUR WOMAN A VAGINAL MASSAGE. This is pretty self-explanatory, but you would set it up similarly to a man's massage (head on pillow, with another pillow under hips, start with deep breathing). Warm her up by starting with the inner thighs or belly. When you get to the area between her legs, start at the outside and work your way in (and up), saving the clitoris for last. Keep the focus on her. This is all about her pleasure. You will probably find this arousing, but do not act on your desires unless she invites you to do so.　♥♥♥♥

252 CONCENTRATE ON THE "TWO LIPS" TECH-NIQUE FOR HER MASSAGE. From Dr. Cadell: "Gently part her outer lips with both of your thumbs and caress them in circular motions for at least two minutes. Next, slide your thumbs up and down her outer lips until they are spread apart, and then do the same with her inner lips. The inner lips are more sensitive than the outer lips, so use less pressure. Watch for her body language and for the swelling of her vaginal lips, which is a natural progression when a woman gets sexually aroused."　♥♥♥

253 MOVE ON TO THE CLITORAL MASSAGE. Gently pull the clitoral hood back from the clitoris to expose it. Then gently slide your thumb and forefinger up and down the sides of the clitoris for about ten strokes. You may feel it growing as it becomes more excited. A clitoris can grow three to four times its normal size when it's fully engorged. Next, massage the head of the clitoris in circular motions using your forefinger or thumb. Don't be surprised if she has a body-melting, earth-shattering orgasm.

254 STIMULATE BOTH SENSITIVE AREAS. Guys, this is something you can work into the vaginal massage (or employ as a separate technique). Once she is sufficiently aroused and/or lubricated, use your thumb to massage her clitoris while using another finger to stimulate her anally. If you are really dexterous, you can also use one of your middle fingers to penetrate her vaginally. It is easier to do this using two hands, but there is something really sexy about the one-handed technique. You feel like you are grasping her entire sensual core in your hand. (Besides, you can always use your other hand to reach up and caress her breasts, for totally mind-blowing, full-body stimulation.)

255 GIVE HIS FEET SOME EROTIC ATTENTION. Stimulate the sole of his foot when he's highly aroused. You can use your tongue, the tips of your fingers, or a feather. A man's soles are the most sensitive part of his foot.

256 WASH YOUR WOMAN'S HAIR. This can be incorporated into a steamy shower or sensual bath, but it is also a good move on its own. Not only is this sweet, it will be very relaxing for her. It can also be a surprisingly sensual and erotic experience for both of you. ♥

257 **TRY OUT SOME OILS AND LOTIONS.** These liquids and lubricants are essential for many sex acts (at least, to make them easier and more comfortable) but they can also add an extra element of excitement. The selection is nearly limitless—you can pick from a ton of different scents (and even flavors). You can also try lotions designed to get warm or hot when massaged on the body. ♥♥♥

258 **MAKE YOUR OWN UNIQUE OIL BLEND.** Here is a great way to make your sexual experience unique: Create your own custom-made massage oil. Do an online search for "recipe" suggestions. Then visit an aromatherapy shop or bath store to pick up some ingredients. Experiment with different combinations until you find a perfect scent (or taste) that both of you love. Your lovemaking will have an added element of excitement as you enjoy basking in your own special blend. ♥♥♥

259 **CHECK OUT STIMULATING CREAMS.** Look for a special type of gel or cream designed specifically to enhance a woman's pleasure. These creams contain an added ingredient that is supposed to create a slight tingling sensation when applied to sensitive areas. The quality and effectiveness of these products can vary

greatly, so try out a few different brands to do your own evaluations. Warning: Start by applying a very tiny amount until you see how it works. Some of these creams can cause a burning sensation that might be uncomfortable.

260 **SUCK ON YOUR PARTNER'S UPPER LIP.** Mark Michaels, author of *Tantra for Erotic Empowerment*, says, "In Tantric anatomy, it is believed that a psychic nerve runs from a woman's upper lip to her genitals and that sucking can be very arousing. We've found that men often have the same response."

261 **SHARE A SEXY SPONGE BATH.** Dr. Cadell recommends a sponge bath as a tender way to achieve sexual pleasure. "It's another way of exploring all those erogenous zones. You can use a warm washcloth or sponge with scented soaps, oils, or gels. Bathing with your lover is much more a part of the sexual practices in many foreign cultures. Bathing is a sweet ritual not only to become clean all over, but to receive a different kind of pleasure as well while stimulating, titillating, and massaging each other's erogenous zones in many ways."

262 **MASTURBATE IN FRONT OF YOUR PARTNER.** A lot of people (especially men) find this really hot. Plus, it also helps them learn more about how you like to be touched. Not to mention, it gives them a break. They can simply lie back and enjoy the show.

263 **MASTURBATE SIMULTANEOUSLY WITH YOUR PARTNER.** This takes all the benefits of masturbating in front of your partner and doubles it. You are each free to do your own thing, while getting off on each other's rising arousal. If you're lucky, you will both manage to climax at the same time.

264 **WATCH A MASTURBATION DEMONSTRATION.** Watch your partner carefully while they masturbate in front of you, and pay close attention to how (and where) they touch themselves. This provides you with some valuable inside information. Keep it in mind during your next sexual encounter.

265 **TREAT YOUR PARTNER TO MANUAL STIMULATION TO THE MAX.** Have a sexual session in which you each try to bring the other person to climax using only your hands. Ladies, this will probably be easy for you—guys often climax from handjobs. Men: take your time, and focus on what you are doing. Avoid just shoving your fingers in there roughly, especially if she is not yet lubricated and ready. Take your time, and practice your "finger fucking" techniques.

266 **BRING YOUR PARTNER TO CLIMAX USING ONLY YOUR MOUTH.** This will be much easier, as most people can reach orgasm fairly easily through oral stimulation. To make things more interesting, give yourself a time limit and see if you can beat the clock.

267 STIMULATE HER (WHILE SHE HELPS). While manually stimulating your woman, gently guide her hand down to that area. Work together using your hands to bring her to a climax. She will love the feeling of pleasuring herself while another hand (or pair of hands) helps. To really bring it home, engage in some deep kissing while both of you stimulate her clitoris and vaginal area manually. You will share an amazing intimate experience, kissing deeply as you bring her to a climax together.

268 STIMULATE HER ORALLY (WHILE SHE HELPS). As your tongue works its magic, guide her hand down to the same spot, prompting her to join the fun. The sensations she gets by pleasuring herself while your tongue dances around the same area will drive her wild.

269 HAVE YOUR PARTNER USE A TOY WHILE GIVING ORAL. While your partner is going down on you, give her a toy to use on herself. This will be exciting for you to watch, and will also provide some unique sensations, as her tongue and mouth will start quivering as she moans or hums. Meanwhile, you get to just lie back and enjoy!

270 GIVE HIM THE BEST ORAL HE'S EVER HAD. Dr. Cadell says, "Most men will agree that they need more pressure on their penis than women are aware of. So ladies, don't be afraid of breaking it. Lavish plenty of attention on the glans (head) with a strong vacuum-style suck. Flicking the frenulum will undoubtedly make him weak in the knees, as will circular motions around the glans; long flat licks up and down the shaft combined with pointy tongue motions bordering the glans will also be welcomed. And don't forget to bestow plenty of oral pleasure around his scrotum."

271 GIVE HER THE BEST ORAL SHE'S EVER HAD.
From Dr. Cadell: "Most women enjoy having their mons kissed, their labia sucked, a talented tongue along the crease where her labia come together. Be observant of her body language as she presses herself against you; slip your tongue inside her vagina, working your way up toward her clitoris. Use your entire tongue, dragging it across her clitoris from the base all the way to the point. Move your tongue from side to side like windshield wipers. Try circular motions as well, both around her clitoris and on it too. Turn your head to the side, alternating again between licking in quick, short strokes and slowly dragging your tongue across her clit from base to point. Don't be afraid to come at her from a different angle!"

272 FIND HER G-SPOT WITH A G-SPOT TOY. Dana Barish of Slumber Parties by Dana says, "Every woman has one, but not everyone can find it, but the ever elusive g-spot is easily located when you have the proper tools. It is one of the strongest and longest orgasms and feels like a wave washing over you. Give a man a tool and he can get the job done."

273 **INTRODUCE HIM TO ANAL.** Men tend to love anal sex when they are the ones doing the penetrating. Being on the receiving end? Now, that's a whole different story. For straight men, the thought of anything even remotely near that area can be uncomfortable, if not downright terrifying. But once they overcome their initial qualms (and their hang-ups about whether enjoying anal means they are secretly gay), a lot of men actually find this very enjoyable. As with anal sex when the woman is the "receiver," the key is to proceed slowly and carefully, and use lots of lubrication.

274 **PLEASURE HIM ON BOTH SIDES.** If your guy agrees to a little anal penetration, take it to the next level by giving him a double dose of pleasure. While stimulating the anal area, use your other hand to reach through (or around) his legs and caress his testicles or shaft.

275 **MAKE THE PERINEUM A PRIORITY.** Your guy has a secret sex spot that you might not even know about. Technically it is called the perineum, but it is also sometimes known as the "sacred spot" or the "million-dollar spot." It is found between the testicles and the anus. This is a sensitive area, so your guy may be nervous about being touched in that spot (and, again, its proximity to the anus may also cause him to be squeamish). But if you can get him to relax and give it a chance, this spot has the potential to provide amazing pleasure. Alternate the type and amount of pressure and stimulation you apply to this area until you find just the right combination he likes.

276 **LADIES, GIVE ANAL A CHANCE.** Sure, it isn't everyone's cup of tea—many women don't even want to consider it. But it can feel amazing for guys, and most men harbor a secret urge to do it with their partners, so think about giving it a try. Granted, you may not love it as much as other sex acts, but you just might like it more than you expected. The key is to go very slowly as you get accustomed to it. Your guy can start off penetrating you with his finger or a sex toy to help you ease your way up to the penile penetration. Use a lot of lubrication (make sure it is compatible with the type of condom you are using, if any). The risk factor depends on whether you are the man or the woman.

277 **TRY ANAL SEX WITH A VIBRATOR ON THE CLITORIS.** Dana Barish shares a few tips: "The key to anal sex is using a good lubricant. Try a lubricant made with silicone so it never dries out. The second key to anal sex is for the recipient to 'push out.' Just like you are pushing something out. Then take a small vibrator and place it on her clitoris during the penetration. Everyone has a happy ending this way."

278 TRY ANAL BEADS. This is a sex toy consisting of a string of smooth beads that can be used along with (or as an alternative to) anal sex. Often the string will contain different sizes, going from smaller to larger. You gradually insert them into the anus—again, lubrication is important—and then pull them out as slowly or quickly as you like. Experiment to find out what you prefer. Many women (and some men) like having the beads removed quickly just as they are climaxing.

279 DO THE DAY-LONG TEASE. Start the morning with some nibbles and kisses before you get out of bed. Tell him just exactly how good he's going to get it later, but make him wait. Fondle him at breakfast. Slip a nasty note in his pocket. Call him at work with throaty reminders. Pick him up from work, naked under an overcoat. Let him look, but don't let him touch. Tease him through dinner. Then wear him out.

280 FOR THE WOMEN. Get (physically) prepared beforehand. Michaels and Johnson suggest you "prime the pump" by pleasuring yourself (slightly) to get your juices flowing an hour before he walks through the door. The more turned on you are before you start, the more you can turn him on.

281 USE EROTIC OILS WITHOUT USING YOUR HANDS. Try having fun with massage oils in a creative way. See if you can massage your partner without using your hands. Any other part of the body is available to be used—but the rule stays the same. No hands!

282 **HAVE SOME WATER FUN WITH A MASSAGING SHOWERHEAD.** Sharing a shower is sexy enough, but you can make it even more exciting. Install a massaging showerhead with a long-reaching flexible hose, and have a little fun soaping up and rinsing your partner. (The massaging showerhead comes in handy for solo showers as well.)

283 **LET YOUR PARTNER GO ON A SEXY TATTOO SCAVENGER HUNT.** Cover yourself with a bunch of temporary tattoos (be sure to put them on strategic places of your body). Be nonchalant about them until the first one is discovered, then let your partner go on a search to try and find the rest.

284 **FIND HER "ELIXIR FIELD."** This is also known as the g-spot from the outside. Tease her with gentle touches just below the navel and above the pubic bone, or let the palm of your warm hand rest there. The touch will give her a heightened state of arousal.

285 **USE AN ICICLE IN AN EROTIC WAY.** Rub it against your partner's naked body (especially those erogenous zones). Don't hold it in a single spot too long, as the cold can get uncomfortable. See how quickly you can make it melt.

286 STUDY UP ON SEX TOYS. This tip is mainly for the guys. Do this before hitting the bedroom, to make yourself a bit more relaxed around toys. Your woman will gladly give you the 411 on how they work, but you can impress her with your sex savvy if you know a few things already. Don't worry, this is one type of homework you will actually enjoy. Study a few sex toy catalogs (or websites) to get familiar with the lingo. Here's one tip: A dildo is designed for penetration, whereas a vibrator is geared towards clitoral stimulation—although many toys combine the two.

287 USE A SEX TOY WHILE YOUR PARTNER WATCHES. Watching your partner pleasure herself can be very exciting, especially for guys. Using a sex toy on yourself while your partner watches can also be a big turn-on. The important thing is not to make your partner think he or she is being replaced. This isn't a substitute for intercourse, it is simply a "side dish." By allowing him to watch you use the sex toy, you give him valuable insight into how you like to be touched. Eventually you can allow him to help you use the sex toy, making it a sex act you can share.

288 USE A SEX TOY THAT YOUR PARTNER PURCHASED. Now that you have allowed your partner to watch you use a sex toy, takes things to the next level by letting her buy you a toy of her choosing. Give her free reign, within reason. (You might want to set down a few rules—say, if you don't feel comfortable with certain types of toys, or don't want anything that might be painful.) Show her your appreciation by allowing her to watch you get off by using the toy. 🔥🔥🔥

289 **USE A SEX TOY DESIGNED FOR TWO.** You can find lots of sex toys designed to be used by a couple together. They include vibrating cock rings that also include a clit stimulator. Another option is a two-headed dildo, so he can experience anal penetration while you are also being penetrated. 🔥🔥🔥

290 **HAVE SEX WITH A VIBRATOR INSERTED AT THE SAME TIME.** From Dana Barish: "For a unique spin on your sex, try inserting a jelly vibrator in along with your penis for a really exciting experience. Lube everything up and enjoy the ride." 🔥🔥🔥

291 **TRY SOME NIPPLE ACCESSORIES.** This is technically for the ladies, but it is something both of you will enjoy. You have a wide variety of nipple accessories to choose from, depending on your comfort level and tastes. Start off with pasties or tassels, and maybe work your way up to nipple jewelry or clamps. 🔥🔥🔥

292 **MAKE YOUR OWN NIPPLE ACCESSORIES.** Be creative! Try out lots of different material, and see which ones look (and feel) the best. 🔥🔥🔥

293 **GET YOUR NIPPLE(S) PIERCED.** If you are really brave (and have a high tolerance for pain) think about

getting a nipple piercing. This can work for either guys or girls.

294 **ENGAGE IN SOME SEXY "SHRIMPING."** Dr. Cadell says: "The foot fetish is one of the most common and has its own slang terminology, 'shrimping,' because to a toe worshiper they look like little shrimp all in a row. Feet have a tremendous number of very sensitive nerve endings. Incorporating footplay into lovemaking can foster intimacy and trust. Pay attention to your lover's feet and toes by kissing, caressing, licking, or sucking all of them."

295 **BREAK OUT THE WHIPPED CREAM.** Whipped cream is the all-purpose sex accessory. Guys, you can use it to decorate your shaft (so of course your girl can lick it off). You can also spray it on your woman and lick it off her. It can work just about anywhere—on bellies, backsides, breasts, you name it.

296 **LICK YOUR PARTNER'S FINGERS IN A SEXY, TANTALIZING WAY.** This technique can be very erotic, especially if you do it very slowly while your partner watches. The power of suggestion plays a role here. They will of course be imagining what else you could do with that talented tongue of yours!

297 **SUCK YOUR PARTNER'S FINGERS.** Now that you have teased your partner's fingers with your tongue, take it a step further and gently suck her fingers. (Watch

out for sharp fingernails or jewelry.) Again, your partner will find this exciting because she will be filled with thoughts of other possibilities. 🖤

298 SUCK YOUR PARTNER'S TOES. This idea is not everyone's favorite, but some people really like it. To make sure your partner's toes are as tasty as possible, do this while the two of you are in the tub during a scented bath (or immediately afterward). 🖤

299 LICK THE BACK OF YOUR PARTNER'S KNEES. This is a sensitive area, and a hidden erogenous zone that many people do not know about. Keep in mind, though—it is also an area that, for many people, is highly ticklish. So be prepared for some giggling or squirming. 🖤

300 KISS OR LICK THE BACK OF YOUR PARTNER'S ANKLES. This is another erogenous zone that is often overlooked. And again, it's a sensitive/ticklish area. Also, some people are self-conscious about their feet in general and might be uncomfortable if their partner spends too much time focusing on them. 🖤

301 USE A HANDHELD FAN TO PROVIDE A THRILL. Use a small handheld fan to cast a cool breeze across your partner's naked body. It will feel good, especially if the room is very warm. The fan may also come in handy for yourself, should you work up a sweat during an intense sexual encounter. 🖤

302 GO IN SEARCH OF YOUR PARTNER'S HOT SPOTS. Dr. Cadell says, "The best way to find your lover's erogenous zones is to give him a sensual massage from head to toe and ask him to rate all your caresses and kisses on a pleasure rating scale from 1 to 10. Don't be offended if your lover rates a kiss on the neck as a 5 and a caress on the thighs as a 7, because everyone has different sensitivity spots. Remember to be creative: Lick your lover's eyebrows, kiss your lover's nose, tongue his lips, nibble your way around his neck, suck on his earlobes and toes. Make sure you don't ignore any moles, freckles, scars, or imperfections either. Next time, it will be your turn to be the receiver of pleasure while your lover explores all your hot spots."

303 GOOSE YOUR PARTNER IN PUBLIC. Pat or grab your partner's ass when the two of you are out in public. It will be an unexpected surprise, and will get his hopes up that something more is awaiting him when you get home. (If your partner is the shy or easily embarrassed type, do this on the sly, when nobody is watching.)

304 MASSAGE YOUR PARTNER'S BODY—WITH YOUR BODY. A tip from Mark Michaels, author of *Tantra for Erotic Empowerment*: "Have your partner lie face down and apply copious amounts of warm oil all over your body (this will be messy). Use your whole naked body to massage your beloved, undulate, writhe, and grind; this is sure to get both of you hot."

305 **LADIES, TRY TO SWALLOW.** Or at least, don't spit (noticeably). If you must spit, do it as discreetly as possible. Or, try to find a compromise, such as allowing him to climax on your face but not in your mouth. (The facial climax also allows him to enact a scene he has probably scene in porn films a million times, which will make him feel like an X-rated stud.)

306 **DO THE DEEP THROAT TECHNIQUE.** Give it a try, at least a few times. This feels amazing to a guy (and they also love watching you do it). Some women find it tough to do without the gagging reflex kicking in, but a little bit of practice—and perhaps some adjustments in position and technique—makes it easier.

307 **BE NICE TO "THE BOYS."** I cannot stress this enough: Whenever you are anywhere near your man's sensitive areas, be careful around the testicles. It goes without saying that you should never ever have anything sharp or rough in that region (unless of course your guy is into that sort of thing).

308 **BE REALLY NICE TO "THE BOYS."** It's great to be careful around the testicles, but it's even better to give them some special attention of their own. Caress them with your tongue. Lick them or suck them (gently). Let your partner be your guide—some men can handle it when you get a little rough down there, while others are more sensitive.

309 **PULL ON HIS BOYS—GENTLY AND AT THE RIGHT TIME.** You will probably need to do a little experimentation to figure out exactly how and when your man likes a little tugging (if at all). Many men enjoy it when their partner tugs—gently!—on their testicles during sex. Giving a soft tug just as your man is about to climax can often intensify the orgasm.

310 **DO SOME HUMMING.** Humming while he is in your mouth can create an amazing vibrating sensation. It does not have to be complicated—just a simple "hmmm" will do. (Even a deep moan would have the same effect.) For added fun, see if you can hum a tune he will recognize.

311 **GO HOT OR COLD FOR AN ADDED ORAL THRILL.** Drinking something cold or warm (not too hot) right before giving him oral can add a delightful twist to the action. You can alternate between both. It also helps ensure your mouth is moist. Good choices might be tea or some kind of minty drink.

312 **JUST ADD ICE TO ORAL OR OTHER FORE PLAY.** When it comes to foreplay, ice can be nice. Rub it on or on your partner's sensitive areas. (Don't hold the ice in one spot for a prolonged period of time, as that can be uncomfortable.) Or, put the ice in your mouth before or during oral sex. The chill will send tingles through your partner's body.

313 **VARY YOUR FELLATIO TECHNIQUE.** The key to giving a great blowjob is to keep your partner guessing. Don't just stick to the same old technique you always use. Start off going fast and then—just as he's reaching his peak—slow things down. Or vice versa.

314 **GO MINTY FOR YOUR MAN.** Sucking on a mint—either before or during oral—can provide your man with a cool tingling sensation. Use caution and proceed slowly, though, as some men find a really strong mint sensation to be unpleasant. (Also, avoid having any really tiny mints in your mouth when giving oral, as they can become lodged in small holes or openings on your partner's body.)

315 **MASTER THE ART OF THE SWIRL.** This is a technique both men and women can add to their repertoire. Ladies, practice doing a swirling motion with your tongue while giving your man oral. This is especially effective near the head of the penis, where the heightened sensitivity makes the swirl feel amazing. Guys, you can do the swirl, too, the next time you give your partner oral. Vary the intensity of pressure to make this even more exciting.

316 **DO THE TWIST.** For the women: When stroking your man, you probably use an up-and-down hand movement. To mix things up, try twisting your hand back and forth around his member, especially at the base. Start out gently until you gauge how forceful your man

likes it. This is also a good move to do while performing oral.

317 **FOLLOW HIS "PRIVATE LINE."** If you look carefully at your guy's private parts, you will notice a line that runs from between his testicles up along his shaft. It's usually a ridge, often visible by a dark line. Trace this path slowly with your tongue, and watch your guy go wild.

318 **DO A DIFFERENT KIND OF DOGGIE STYLE.** Dr. Cadell says, "It's nice to know that this position is conducive to more than just intercourse. It's actually a great angle for receiving oral sex, both for men and women. Focus on his pleasure as he gets into doggie pose on his hands and knees with his legs spread apart. By drawing his penis back between his legs, he can now be lavishly licked and sucked by his partner."

319 **USE YOUR TONGUE—TO LICK MORE THAN USUAL.** When performing oral sex on your man, don't just use your lips and mouth. Take your time with the tongue action. Let your tongue run up and down his entire length, slowly. Gradually increase the speed and intensity of your tongue movements.

320 **USE YOUR TONGUE—TO TICKLE HIM WITH DELIGHT.** Flick your tongue back and forth quickly in certain sensitive areas (for example, the underside of

the head of his penis). If you have good tongue control, try fluttering it like a butterfly to give him a sensation that will make him shudder.

321 **GIVE HIM HEAD—UPSIDE DOWN.** Lie on your back on the bed, with your head leaning over the side. Have him approach the bed, and take him into your mouth (you might need to lift your head a little bit). This will give him a great vantage point, and will also allow him to see and touch your breasts.

322 **RAISE HER (LOWER HALF) UP WHILE PER-FORMING ORAL.** The man should kneel on the bed, with the woman lying on her back in front of him. The man lifts her up from under her ass, bring her waist up to his face. The woman can then wrap her legs around his head. This allows the man easy access for deep tongue penetration, and also lets him stimulate her anally while giving oral.

323 **TRY TEA-BAGGING.** This term means to put a man's scrotum into his partner's mouth, usually while the man is on top and can then thrust or bounce up and down. Have the woman lie on the bed with her head raised on pillows. The man gets on all fours above her so that his groin is above her face. Start out gently while gauging the man's comfort level.

324 **EXPLORE HER FROM BEHIND.** She lies down on her belly, with you behind her, kneeling by her waist.

You can explore her—visually and manually—as much as you want, and she cannot turn her head to look back. This technique allows the element of surprise since she doesn't know what you will do next. Plus, you are free to check her out without being self-conscious that she's watching.

325 **EXPLORE HIM FROM BEHIND.** It's her turn to look at you, so switch places. Resist your guy tendencies to be uptight about anyone exploring your rear end.

326 **GLOW IN THE DARK.** Buy a black light, and use washable marker (or better yet, some type of bright edible food) to draw a trail on your partner or mark their "special spots." Turn the lights off, and use the black light to make the marks glow in the dark.

327 **GIVE HER A BUZZ DURING ORAL.** Guys, try this trick that is guaranteed to be a hit: While performing oral sex on your partner, place a small vibrator under your chin or beside your cheek. This will add a thrilling humming sensation to the action that will drive your woman wild.

328 **GIVE HIM A BUZZ DURING ORAL.** Ladies, now it is your turn to return the favor. Place a vibrator on the outside of your face or under your chin while performing oral sex on your man. Do not give your partner any advance notice. He will love this stimulating surprise.

329 GIVE HIS BOYS A BUZZ WHILE PERFORMING ORAL. Just because your mouth is occupied elsewhere, that doesn't mean his balls have to be neglected. Use a vibrating sex toy (a small one would probably work best) to stimulate his testicles while your mouth takes care of his penis. It's a two-for-one bonus!

330 ADD A VIBRATING RING WHILE PERFORMING ORAL. Your guy probably thinks oral sex couldn't possibly get any better, but he is in for a big surprise. Take your basic blowjob to the next level by putting a vibrating penis ring on him first. His brain (and body) will be spinning as he enjoys two different pleasures at once.

331 IMITATE ORAL TECHNIQUES. When it comes to oral sex (whether on a man or a woman), there are lots of different techniques—some more popular and/or effective than others. Watch some adult films together, paying close attention to any oral tricks or techniques you see. Then make a game out of trying to imitate the different techniques you have seen. Not all of them will be hits, but you will have fun experimenting.

332 TALK DIRTY. This tip can be especially effective when coming from a woman. Just uttering a few key words (say, "throbbing cock" or "hot, wet pussy") can send your guy over the edge. And it can be particularly powerful if you aren't usually the type of girls who uses dirty words. Your guy will consider it a compliment, as if his bedroom skills have brought out such passion in you that you unleashed your inner vixen. It will probably be a real ego boost for him. Plus, he will love hearing you talk dirty.

333 TALK REALLY DIRTY. We're talking straight out of the filthiest porn mag you can find. Just be sure your partner is up to it. If you've let loose with some really raunchy talk, it can make for an awkward moment if your partner suddenly recoils in shock.

334 FILL IN THE BLANKS. If you're having trouble coming up with some X-rated things to say, Dr. Cadell suggests using these fill-in-the-blank examples: "It feels so good when you touch my _____." "Your _____ is beautiful." "I want you to _____ my _____." "I love your _____." "My _____ is so _____."

335 TELL HIM WHAT TO DO. Most men really want to please their partners. Really, they do. And they are usually willing to do just about anything to accomplish that goal. The problem is, they aren't mind readers. Frankly, they often aren't even very good at reading subtle hints or little clues. The solution: Give clear instructions. Keep it succinct and boil it down to simple commands like "harder," "faster," "move up here," or things like that. Don't worry about being bossy. Most likely, he will be grateful for the guidance. (Besides, many men secretly want to be bossed around in bed, at least a little bit, anyway.)

336 MAKE YOUR PARTNER BEG FOR IT. Torture your partner a little bit (in a fun way). Tease them and "play" with them, but don't give her intercourse, or whatever she really wants at that moment. Tantalize her with sexy little moves until she can't stand it. Refuse to give her what she wants until she literally begs for it—or at least says "please" a few times really sincerely. You don't want to make her beg for it all the time, of course, but it is nice to know at least once that someone wanted you so much that she was willing to beg.

337 BEG YOUR PARTNER FOR WHAT YOU WANT— EVEN IF HE DOES NOT MAKE YOU. Show him you simply cannot stand to wait one more minute of this torture. You want—no, you need—him on you (or inside of you) right now—please!

338 FORCE YOUR PARTNER TO TALK DIRTY. If she is reluctant to use dirty words, this can help get her off the hook. (Hey, you forced her into it. It's not like she wanted to or anything.) Give her instructions. For example: "I want you to tell me to lick your pussy. And I won't do it until you say those words." Chances are, she will be cursing like a sailor before you know it.

339 GIVE HER AN ORGASM IN THE SHOWER. Krista Bloom, Ph.D., clinical sexologist and relationship expert, shares these tips: "Kneel or squat in the shower under her. Spread her legs apart about 6 inches. Lick the insides of her thighs, being sure to start from the sides, and then move your tongue and mouth onto her outer labia (lips). Lick up and down on her labia. Then move away to her stomach or legs. Place your hands around her waist and back to support her. Then move your tongue in a circle around her clitoris. After a few minutes, gently insert one finger into her vaginal canal about an inch and hold it there. This should drive her wild! Give her the screaming orgasm she deserves without demanding your own pleasure in return."

340 GIVE HIM AN ORGASM IN THE SHOWER. Bloom's tips: "Kneel or squat in the shower under him. Place one hand around his waist and back to support him. Place your other hands underneath his testicles, lifting them gently and tickling or rubbing them with your fingers. Lick the sides (shaft) of his penis firmly with your tongue. Do this for at least a minute or two, while still holding his testicles. Then lick the head or top of the penis, circling it with your tongue. Look up at him during the action, which can be an extra turn-on. Begin sucking on his member until it fills your mouth. Continue to play underneath with your fingers while you suck on him. Allow him to explode in your mouth, or, when you know he is about to come, stroke his head and shaft vigorously with your hand, keeping his penis close to your face so he can come on you. Remember,

you are in the shower, so you can wash off right then and there."

341 USE CODE WORDS AND SIGNALS FOR YOUR ROUGH PLAY. It's like having your own intimate language, and ensures that both of you know when to stop if your partner becomes uncomfortable.

342 MAKE YOUR PARTNER A PASSION PRISONER. Bloom says this is a great way for S&M-curious couples to try out some bondage moves. "Tell your lover she is going to be your prisoner of love for the hour. The object of this game is to try something new and to find some new pleasure zones. Use silk or satin scarves, or any other type of soft material to tie up your lover. Then, start exploring their body, allowing the sensory deprivation of being unable to see heighten her other senses."

343 TEASE YOUR PRISONER WITH FOOD. Feed your blindfolded prisoner sensual foods such as grapes, ice cream, your finger dipped in chocolate, or strawberries dipped in whipped cream. Be sure to go slow, to tease her with the food to prolong the experience.

344 SLOWLY PLEASURE YOUR PRISONER. Use a feather to sensually tickle your lover's arms, legs, body, and face. Sensually touch her all over, saving the genital play for last. You can also use a small vibrating toy to stimulate your lover's genitals to orgasm while she is

your captive. Start out circling the surrounding areas of the pelvis. Use circular motions to stimulate both male and female genitals. You can also use your mouth on your lover's genitals until your lover reaches orgasm.
💙💙💙💙

345 **T**REAT HIM LIKE A GOD FOR AN ENTIRE DAY. For once, let him feel what it's like to have someone worship at his feet (literally, if you're willing). Wait on him hand and foot. More importantly, treat his body with reverence and view sex as a sacred event. He will feel like Zeus! 💙💙💙

346 **T**REAT HER LIKE A GODDESS FOR THE DAY. Worship her beauty. Let her know she is your idea of feminine perfection, heaven on earth. You can be her male slave, ready to do whatever she wishes. 💙💙💙

347 **C**REATE YOUR VERY OWN SEXUAL RITUAL CEREMONY. Picture the ceremonies described in *The DaVinci Code*, where chosen women had sex with an exalted leader while everyone else watched and chanted. Make your ceremony as elaborate as possible. For added excitement, try to add an air of secrecy or mystery. 💙💙💙

348 **H**AVE A TWENTY-FOUR-HOUR FOREPLAY MARATHON. Spend an entire day engaging in fore-play. (Weekends or a day when you don't have to work would be best.) Make every interaction with your partner as sensual as possible. Be creative—see how many different foreplay ideas you can come up with. But take it no further than foreplay until the twenty-four hours are done.

349 **TRY ONE NEW FOREPLAY TECHNIQUE EACH TIME.** Take turns coming up with the new trick. See how long you can go without running out of ideas.

350 **GIVE WITHOUT EXPECTATIONS.** Foreplay is not a tit-for-tat (no pun intended) type of thing. Ideally, you should both find every act of foreplay enjoyable— whether you are on the "giving" or "receiving" end, or both. You should never get to the point of thinking (or, worse, saying), "Okay, we spent ten minutes on 'your' foreplay—now it's my turn!" Of course, if it gets to the point where your foreplay almost always focuses on one person, and the other person starts to feel neglected, then you may need to make some adjustments. Otherwise, think of this as something that benefits both of you.

Chapter 8

Porn

Porn has gotten a bad rap—it has been blamed for everything under the sun. And, it's true, pornography and the adult entertainment industry as a whole have some downsides. But when it comes to adding some heat to your sex life, porn can come in pretty damn handy. It's fast, reliable, and efficient. And it's versatile—you can find a type of porn that suits you, no matter what your preferences, fetishes, or sexual quirks. It's easily accessible and can be ordered or obtained from the privacy of your own home.

Porn can provide a boost to a lagging libido or a sex life gone stale. If you have the right approach, you can use porn to improve and enhance your relationship with your partner. Some keys: Don't become so reliant on porn that it replaces "real" sex, or you find yourself unable to become aroused without it. Also, never compare yourself or your partner to anyone you see on a porn tape or adult magazine. That's just asking for trouble.

351 **VENTURE INTO NEW TERRITORY.** So, you have never been to an adult store? Just go—don't think about it, just do it. Take a friend if that helps. There's no need to venture into the seedy side of town—many upscale adult chains have locations in safe suburban areas. 💕💕

352 **DON'T JUST WINDOW SHOP.** Vow to buy at least three new things you have never tried before. Try not to overthink it. Impulse shopping is a good thing in this case. And don't let your new purchases sit unopened in a drawer—the goal is to actually use them. 💕💕

353 **BE GENEROUS WHEN SHOPPING AT AN ADULT STORE.** Buy something for your partner—something that is for his pleasure. Allow him privacy to check it out on his own, if he wishes. If you're lucky, he will invite you to watch a demonstration. 💕💕💕

354 **DO YOUR ADULT SHOPPING ONLINE.** No adult store in your area? No problem. You can easily order adult products online from a site like *www.adamandeve.com* (stick with reputable, well-known sites to lessen the risk of credit card fraud or other problems). Don't worry about your nosy mailman—most companies ship the products in discreet packaging. 💕💕

355 **GET SOME SEX TOY SURPRISES.** If you are really feeling adventurous, go to an online adult toy site and order three things just based on the product name

alone, without reading the descriptions. Then get your partner to do the same. You will have fun when the package arrives and you discover the surprises inside. ♥♥♥

356 GO TO A SEX TOY PARTY. These are the modern-day, sexy versions of Tupperware parties. You can see (and feel) the products—and get a crash course in how they all work—in a fun, relaxed setting. Don't worry—you place your order privately, so nobody else knows what you're buying. ♥♥

357 JOIN YOUR PARTNER AT A SEX TOY PARTY. Go to a coed sex toy party so you can both check out the products (and order some new toys) together. If nothing else, you will have fun playing the party games. ♥♥♥

358 BRING THE PARTY TO YOU. Better yet, host your own toy party. You will still have fun, plus you will earn some free toys! Invite a diverse group of people—include the shy types, and maybe you can help them break out of their shell. Serve liquor at the party to help people loosen up. ♥♥♥

359 BUY PORN MAGS TOGETHER—AT A STORE WHERE THEY KNOW YOU. Sure, you can order your porn so it arrives directly in your mailbox, but it's much more daring to go buy the magazines in person. Next time you're at the local store, spend some time at the porn rack and pick out a few enticing choices. Then pretend not to notice the funny glances the clerk shoots your way when you check out.

360 **MAKE A TAPE OF YOURSELVES HAVING SEX.** By now, we are all well aware of where this could lead. But it can still be exciting. If you do make a sex tape, watch it a few times—and then erase it. And never let it out of your sight.

361 **WATCH GIRL-ON-GIRL ACTION.** Check out a porn tape featuring two women together. Whether you are a man or a woman, it's probably something you have thought about or pictured in your mind. This is your chance to see if it lives up to all the hype.

362 **WATCH A GANG BANG (ON TAPE).** Even if a gang bang is not your taste, everyone should see a gang bang at least once—if for no other reason, just to gaze in awe at the endurance abilities involved. You may start to feel sore and/or exhausted just watching.

363 **WATCH A TAPE FEATURING YOUR FANTASY.** If you can find a tape featuring one or more of your fantasy scenarios, check it out. The viewing will help you determine if it really is something you're interested in—and just might give you a few new ideas.

364 **CREATE YOUR OWN PORN STORYLINE.** If you're like most people, you find the plots (and, worse,

the dialogue—or lack thereof) of most porn flicks laughable. Think you can do better? Try to create your own premise for a film, complete with plot and dialogue.
❤❤❤❤

365 **MAKE YOUR OWN (SCRIPTED) PORN TAPE.** Now that you have a plot for the next X-rated blockbuster, try to actually capture it on tape. You and your partner can be the stars, or you can enlist the help of some brave friends. You might even decide it is good enough to sell (although that presents a bunch of other issues you need to consider). ❤❤❤❤

366 **MAKE A TAPE OF SOMEONE ELSE HAVING SEX** ... with their knowledge and consent, of course. A few factors make this idea challenging, however. First, you either need to wait for someone to ask you to be his cameraman, or broach the idea yourself. Second, you need to know the person/people very well in order to feel comfortable. In a way, though, if you do know them well, it might be even more awkward. (Filming your best friend having sex? Ew.) You also need to consider the possibility that you might find the action to be very arousing—how will you handle that? (Stop filming, drop the camera and run? Try to join the action?) The risk factor depends on who the "actors" are. ❤❤❤

367 **WATCH A CELEBRITY SEX TAPE.** Admit it, the curiosity is killing you. Plus, you really want to know if they have (or do) something you don't. You might be

surprised—or possibly even relieved—to discover they don't know any magic tricks. For the most part, they have sex just like us regular folks.

368 WRITE YOUR OWN PORN. Go somewhere quiet with a notebook and pencil (or a laptop, if you prefer). Play some sensual music, if that helps establish the proper mood. Write a steamy short story, and then submit it to a website or literary publication that specializes in erotica.

369 SPEND A WEEK CONDUCTING YOUR OWN PRIVATE ADULT FILM FESTIVAL. Watch as many different types of porn movies as you can. Be sure to include some that you wouldn't normally pick. Expand your erotic horizons, and you might be shocked to discover some unexpected turn-ons.

370 DEVISE YOUR OWN ADULT MOVIE RATINGS SYSTEM. You could try a "four stars" type of ratings system or something more complex. Maybe you will assign a certain number of points for each act of penetration, each different sex toy, or whatever. You and your partner will enjoy sharing this inside joke when trying to decide which adult movie to buy or watch.

371 BECOME AN ONLINE PORN CRITIC. Scout the help wanted sites for gigs. Believe it or not, some people actually watch porn for a living. If nothing else, you might get some free movies. If you can't find a gig, simply start your own blog or site on which you share your critiques and reviews. You might soon develop a loyal following.

372 CHECK OUT THE ADULT FILMS MADE ESPE-CIALLY FOR WOMEN. You can find porn movies made by women, for women. These films tend to have a stronger focus on romance and plot. One example is the Candida Royale series. Also, Stella Films (a woman-owned company) is another good choice, as they specialize in films featuring women in strong roles.

373 WATCH SOME AMATEURS ON FILM. There is a entire category of porn devoted especially to films made by amateurs. They may lack the recognizable names and fancy sets of the professional porn flicks, but watching amateurs can be surprisingly exciting. Bonus: These people actually look real, like you or someone you know. If you tend to get self-conscious watching professional porn stars (That perfect hair! Those surgically enhanced breasts!), you might feel more comfortable watching amateurs on screen.

374 PLAY AN X-RATED VIDEO GAME. Think video games are just for kids? Then you haven't checked out the "adult" variety—such as Virtually Jenna, an interactive X-rated video game featuring porn star Jenna Jameson. It's like having online sex—without the cheating.

375 **WATCH AN ALL-MALE DANCE REVUE.** This is for the ladies. Your man probably won't want to join you as you watch the sexy male dancers. But a smart guy will encourage you to enjoy the show, knowing he will reap the benefits when you get home. Chances are, you will be all hot and bothered—and in need of someone to finish off what the dancers started. 💗💗

376 **WATCH SOME NUDE MALE DANCERS.** Again, this is for the ladies—but their male partners can enjoy the benefits. 💗💗💗💗

377 **CHECK OUT A "FORUM" OR "FANTASIES" SECTION.** Almost every adult magazine has this section, and the stories range from laughable to downright shocking. See if they give you any ideas of new things you would like to try. 💗💗💗

378 **TAKE TURNS READING THE FANTASY STORIES TO EACH OTHER OUT LOUD.** You can be silly, sexy, or serious. Then take turns guessing whether you think any of the "confessions" are actually true. You might even get a kick out of imagining the person who wrote the story, and what they really look or act like. 💗💗💗

379 **ALLOW YOUR PARTNER TO PICK OUT A FANTASY STORY.** The two of you will try to recreate it. You may not be able to successfully pull it off, but you will probably have fun trying. And then it is your turn

to make the selection, and your partner must help you act it out.

380 WRITE A LETTER ABOUT ONE OF YOUR OWN ESCAPADES (OR FANTASIES). Send it in. If nothing else, it will get your creative juices flowing (and may put you in the mood for romance). Who knows, you just might see it in print. Just be sure not to use your real name.

381 BUY SEX TOYS FOR YOUR FRIENDS. They may be too shy to buy sex toys themselves. What are friends for? Pick out a really good toy, and send it to them (if you think they would be embarrassed if you gave it to them in person). Be willing to share tips on how to use it.

382 ASK FOR SEX TOY RECOMMENDATIONS. The next time you visit an adult store, ask the employees what they recommend. If you're lucky, they just might clue you in on a brand-new item, or point you to an older product you had never noticed.

383 GIVE RECOMMENDATIONS. If you have amassed a wealth of sex toy knowledge, share the wealth. If any of your friends show the slightest interest in spicing up their sex lives, offer tips and suggestions for the latest sex toys they might want to try.

CHAPTER 9

POSITIONS

Once you have enjoyed your fair share of foreplay, it's time to get down to business and focus on the "main course." As in, intercourse. Penetration. Banging. Fucking. Whatever you call it, you probably consider this the main event. If you are like most couples, this is likely to be the time when you fall into your tried-and-true routine. Most people have a few positions that they like to stick with. They figure, "Hey, if it works, why change?" Well, for the same reason that there is more than one choice on a restaurant menu—even a delicious entrée gets boring if you have the same thing over and over again.

Nobody is saying you need to ditch your favorite positions. But try to add some excitement by testing out a few new ones. You just might find a few new favorites! Here are a bunch of suggestions to get you started—but be creative, use your imagination, and see if you can come up with a few of your own inventions.

384 TRY THE YAB YUM POSE. This is an ancient lovemaking position in which both partners are sitting. First, the man sits with his legs crossed and pulled in (picture the typical yoga meditation pose). Then the woman sits on top of him, facing him, and wraps her legs around his back, almost as if you are intertwined in an intimate hug. This position doesn't allow for much movement, but encourages closeness and also supposedly allows for harmony of the couple's chakras (the life forces that run up and down the body).

385 HAVE SEX WHILE SITTING IN THE SAME DIRECTION. The man sits down first (either on a couch or bed, or in a chair). The woman, with her back toward him, lowers herself onto him so that she is essentially sitting on his lap. She can then bounce up and down on top of him as he thrusts into her.

386 SIT AND STRADDLE. This is another sitting position, but this time, the man sits down and the woman straddles him so that they are facing each other. The woman would support her weight on her knees, which allows her to raise and lower herself onto the man. This is the basic position you would use to have sex in a car (or perhaps a plane or other vehicle), if the man was sitting down and the woman wanted to mount him.

387 CONQUER THE KAMA SUTRA. Work your way through every position in the *Kama Sutra*. It is probably the most famous of all the sex books, and based on ancient techniques. Some of the positions are included here, but there are lots more for you to try.

388 PURSUE MORE TANTRIC WISDOM, IF YOU LIKE. For more ancient mystical guidance when it comes to sex advice and techniques that have been passed down through the centuries, you should check out (shameless plug alert!) *The Everything® Tantric Sex Book*, by the author of this book.

389 HAVE SEX IN THE MISSIONARY POSITION. The woman lies down on her back, then the man lies on top of her so that they are face to face. It's very simple, but very popular. Let's face it, the reason it's the most common position is because it works.

390 MAKE THE MISSIONARY POSITION YOUR OWN. Have sex in the missionary position, but try to come up with your own unique twist to add to it. Encourage your partner to give this some thought and make suggestions, too. See how many different variations you can come up with.

391 LIFT YOUR LEGS, LADIES. This adds a little extra excitement to the basic missionary position. Ladies: while your man is on top of you, lift your legs up to the side of your man's arms (so each of your knees is near one of his elbows). This allows for deeper penetration.

392 **LIFT YOUR LEGS HIGHER.** Taking that position ever farther, lift your legs all the way up so that they rest on your man's shoulders. Ladies, you will now almost be folded in half. It may not be comfortable to remain this way for too long, but the ability for really deep penetration will make it worthwhile.

393 **TRY ANOTHER "LEGS UP HIGH" POSITION.** In this position, the woman lies on her back, bringing her bottom to the edge of the bed (or a chair or couch). The man then kneels on the floor in front of her and enters her, lifting her legs up high so her feet are resting on his shoulders. By lifting the woman's legs and bottom up off the bed, the man can do some deep thrusting.

394 **RAISE ONE LEG ONLY.** In a hybrid of the previous two positions, the woman only lifts one leg above the man's shoulder, keeping the other leg flat. This allows for a bit more freedom of movement. Alternate raising each leg, switching them back quickly for a little added friction. Note: In ancient sex tomes, this position is known as "splitting the bamboo."

395 **GIVE THE RAISED MISSIONARY POSITION A TRY.** This is an easy variation of the missionary position. The woman simply lies on her back with some pillows, blankets or other comfy items under her hips, to help raise her pelvic area up a bit (for easier access and better penetration).

396 **T**RY THE FROG POSITION (ALSO KNOWN AS THE LEAPFROG POSITION). In this position, the woman kneels on the bed, with her legs drawn up towards her midsection. The man then kneels or stands behind her and enters her behind. The natural inclination is for the woman to tuck her feet down so that they are flat along the bed, soles up. However, to lift her pelvis a bit higher, she should brace herself with her feet planted on the bed. She would now look almost like she was about to do a frog jump (hence the name of the position). Keeping your feet like that for very long can be uncomfortable, though.

397 **T**RY THE SCISSORS POSITION. This may sound a little tricky, but once you put it into action, you will probably want to do it again and again. The woman and man lie on the bed so that their heads are at opposite ends of the bed. They then intertwine their legs so one of the woman's legs is under the man's, while her other leg is above him. Essentially, his midsection (and one of his legs) is now "clamped" between the woman's legs. By propping himself up on one of his arms, the man can manually stimulate the woman while she has a good view of the action.

398 D**O THE **C**AT TECHNIQUE. The CAT (or coital alignment technique) is a variation on the missionary position. In the normal missionary position, the man's pelvis is usually positioned lower than the woman's, to allow him to enter up into her. With the CAT technique, he moves up toward the head of the bed, so that his pelvis is aligned with hers. This might feel a bit unusual at first—and you might need to be careful that he doesn't slip out (wrap your legs around him to help prevent this)—but it allows for maximum clitoral stimulation.

399 **HAVE SEX WITH THE WOMAN ON TOP.** The basic female-dominant position involves the woman on top of the man with a knee at each side of him, so that she is straddling him. The woman-on-top position is really gaining in popularity. For one thing, many modern women really like being in the "power position." Plus, this allows them to have more control over the movement and speed of your thrusting. Guys, you should love this position too—it provides a great view of (and easy access to) her bouncing breasts, while allowing you to lie back and do less of the work.

400 **STIMULATE YOUR FEMALE PARTNER WHILE SHE IS ON TOP.** For the guys: stimulate her clitoris manually while she rides you.

401 **DO A LITTLE LIFTING.** To make the woman-on-top position pleasurable for both of you, she should lift herself up and down in her own rhythm. If she pulls herself up so that she is almost—but not quite—off of you, and then quickly comes back down for full penetration, it will feel incredible for both of you. (You can

help lift her up and down if she starts to get tired.)
♥♥♥♥

402 COME ON DOWN. If the woman needs to take a break—or just wants to kiss or get close to you—she can learn forward, so that you are face to face. This gives both of you a break, allows for some whispered pillow talk, and switches up the sensation. ♥♥♥

403 RIDE 'EM, COWGIRL. A variation of the woman-on-top position is called the "reverse cowgirl." In this position, the woman spins around so that she is looking at the man's feet. This angle provides a different sensation, and also gives the man easy access for anal stimulation with his fingers. ♥♥♥

404 SWIM LIKE A SEAL. This is another woman-on-top position. This time, the woman lies face down and flat on top of the man, so that her entire body is in a straight line. Their entire bodies are touching. Often, the woman will then raise her head and shoulders up a bit, giving the man easier access to her breasts. The woman would then look kind of like a seal with its head pointed up in the air (hence the name). This is sometimes also called the "swimming" position. ♥♥

405 DO IT DOGGIE-STYLE. Rear-entry (commonly known as "doggie-style") is a must for every couple's sexual repertoire. This position is popular for a variety of reasons. First, it encourages deep penetration and rapid thrusting. At the same time, it allows for manual stimulation of the woman's clitoris (either by herself or her partner). Men really love this position because they can clearly see their penis going in and out of their partner, which is very arousing. Of course, men also tend to appreciate the view of their partner's rear end. Some women don't like the lack of face-to-face inter-action, but the advantages of this position more than compensate for that.

406 ADD AN EXTRA ELEMENT TO DOGGIE-STYLE. Guys, take advantage of the easy access to your partner's ass and seize the opportunity to squeeze, spank, or caress it.

407 HAVE SEX WHILE KNEELING. A popular varia-tion of the doggie-style position involves both part-ners kneeling (either on the bed or the floor), with the man behind the woman. This provides for a little more closeness, but may become uncomfortable for the man after a period of time.

408 TRY DOGGIE-STYLE WITH A DOWNWARD SLANT. A variation of the doggie-style position involves the man entering the woman from behind (as he either stands or kneels behind her) and then the woman bringing her face down closer to the bed or floor. This is often a natural extension of the action after assuming the doggie-style position (many women will often automatically switch to this pose as they come closer to climaxing). This allows for deep penetration, while also allowing the woman to easily reach behind her and caress the man's testicles. Thrusting in this position provides considerable clitoral stimulation, so many women find it easy to climax this way.

409 **H**AVE SEX STANDING FACE-TO-FACE. Having sex while the two of you are standing face-to-face might sound simple, but it can be tricky. It is especially challenging if you and your partner have a big height difference. Plus, it does not really allow for a lot of movement.

410 **S**TAND FACE-TO-FACE (WITH LADY LIFTED). An easier (and more exciting) version of the standing face-to-face version involves the man standing, while the woman is sitting on top of something (say, a desk or counter). Think of any of the famous "doing it in the kitchen" movie scenes. If there is nothing for the woman to sit on, the man can simply lift her up (she can wrap her legs around him to stay in place) and bounce her up and down. This can quickly get tiring for the man, though, so it's usually only efficient for quick encounters.

411 **G**IVE THE WHEELBARROW A WHIRL. If you want to put a doggie-style twist on the standing position, give the wheelbarrow a try. It's not for wimps, though (or people with weak upper arm strength). The man stands behind the woman, who leans down

toward the floor. The man then lifts her legs up toward
his waist and enters her, as the woman supports herself with her hands and arms. Picture a wheelbarrow
race (only with naked participants).

412 HAVE SEX SIDE-BY-SIDE (WHILE SPOONING).
For something new, try having sex side-by-side. There
are a few variations of this basic premise. First, you can
lie in the spooning position (which allows the man to
enter his partner from behind).

413 HAVE SEX WHILE LYING FACE TO FACE. You can
also lie face to face, although that can make intercourse
a bit difficult.

414 HAVE SEX WITH HIM ON HIS SIDE, HER ON
HER BACK. The man lies on his side, with the woman
next to him on her back. She then slides over closer to
him, raising up onto her side a bit, with her legs intertwined with his (her lower leg between his, her upper
leg draped over the top of his). This lets the man enter
her from behind, while keeping her legs far enough
apart to allow for manual stimulation.

415 PUT HER ON TOP, DIAGONALLY. The man lies on
his back, and the woman lies on top of him, on her
belly, so that she is diagonally across his body. See how
far diagonally she can go while still keeping you inside
of her. (It is tougher than it sounds.)

416 NOW TRY HIM ON TOP, DIAGONALLY. The woman lies on the bed, and the man gets on top of her, diagonally. Again, men, see how much you can move while still remaining inside of her. However, stop at the first twinge of pain (twisting too far while you are inside of her wouldn't be a good idea).

417 HAVE SEX IN THE SPREAD-EAGLE POSITION. This is a variation of the missionary position. The woman is on the bottom, but spreads her legs wide open, so her feet are as far apart as possible (perhaps they are way up in the air, or propped up on the headboard or the ends of the couch). This allows for maximum penetration.

418 TRY THE MALE SPREAD-EAGLE POSITION. Now, switch places—putting the man on his back with his legs spread. (Most likely, he won't be able to spread his legs as far apart as she can.) This will give the woman full access to his body, to do whatever she wishes to (and for) him.

419 TRY SEX WHILE SHE IS SPREAD EAGLE AND RESTRAINED. To ensure she stays in the spread-eagle position (or to assist her in staying that way in case she starts to get tired), use some bondage techniques. With her permission, secure her feet to the bedpost or other surface with some scarves or S&M restraints.

420 TRY SEX WHILE HE IS SPREAD EAGLE AND RESTRAINED. This is the male version of the previous maneuver. Make sure he keeps his eyes open as you eye him up, debate what to do with your "captive" and then ultimately make your move. He won't want to miss that sight.

421 GET ON YOUR KNEES TO SERVICE YOUR MAN. Obviously, this is an oral sex position in which the woman performs fellatio on the man while kneeling in front of him. This probably ranks up there as one of a man's favorite positions.

422 CARESS YOUR MAN WHILE ON YOUR KNEES. To give him an added thrill, the woman can reach around and grab or caress his ass while going down on him.

423 LIE DOWN AND ENJOY SOME FELLATIO. When the woman is performing fellatio on her partner, some people like to do it while both are lying down, for the sake of comfort. This also allows the man a better view of the action. A man will often get an added thrill by watching his partner go down on him.

424 LOOK AT HIM WHILE PERFORMING FELLATIO. To get your partner even more aroused, make eye contact while performing fellatio, and make it obvious how much you are enjoying pleasuring him.

425 **PERFORM FELLATIO WHILE HE IS SITTING DOWN.** In this variation of fellatio positions, the man is sitting down (say, on a chair or at the edge of the bed) while the woman kneels in front of him. You would employ this position if engaging in oral sex while in a car or other unusual locations.

426 **PERFORM ORAL SEX ON HER WHILE KNEELING.** When performing oral sex on a woman, a man will sometimes kneel in front of her while she lies on a bed with her legs draped over the side. This provides the man with a good viewpoint and also allows the woman to stimulate herself manually simultaneously.

427 **ENJOY ORAL, WITH WOMAN ON TOP.** The man lies down, and the woman lowers her bottom down to his face (she is basically kneeling above his face, or sitting on top of it). This can get uncomfortable for both parties after a while, so is best for "fast and furious" sessions.

428 **TRY HAVING ORAL SEX IN THE SIXTY-NINE POSITION.** Perhaps one of the most famous sex positions is the one nicknamed the "69" position. The partners lie with their heads pointing in opposite directions, so that the man's face is near the woman's waist and vice versa. They can then perform oral sex on each other simultaneously.

429 **T**RY ANAL SEX, DOGGIE-STYLE. Anal sex positions are generally very similar to the basic vaginal sex positions (except, of course, that the penetration occurs in a different spot). The most common anal sex position is probably the doggie-style technique, with the man kneeling or standing behind the woman. One downside of this anal position is that the woman has very little control over the speed and strength of the thrusting, and the man may quickly find himself getting carried away into his rhythm.

430 **T**RY ANAL LYING ON YOUR SIDE. Another anal sex position features both people lying on their side, with the man behind the woman. The woman may feel more relaxed in this position, because the man is more likely to use slow thrusting movements, and the woman has more control over the pace.

431 **D**O DOUBLE PENETRATION. Men, have sex with your partner as you normally would (meaning, by penetrating her with your penis) while at the same time using a dildo or other toy in her ass. Or switch it around, and use the toy vaginally while having anal sex.

432 **S**EE IF YOU CAN PULL OFF A TRIPLE PENETRATION MOVE. Now, while already doing the double penetration move, stimulate her clitoris with your hand or a sex toy (or have her do it herself). This is a bit tricky and might require some practice.

433 Do the "69" position, but add a toy to the mix. While your female partner is giving you oral, start out by pleasuring her with your mouth—but then finish the job with a sex toy. Bonus: The more you make her moan, the better it will feel for you.

434 Do the "69" position with a toy—by surprise. Let her get comfortable with the "69" position, and start out as you normally do, by giving her oral. Then quietly take out a toy you had hidden under your pillow (or elsewhere nearby) beforehand. Give her a surprise thrill. Her sudden gasp or moan—while she has your shaft in her mouth—will send shivers through you.

435 The "just pull 'em down" position. This is not exactly an official position per se, but it is the position couples usually find themselves in when engaging in a quickie. Basically, the woman leans over a piece of furniture, a counter or whatever happens to be nearby (or she simply props herself against a wall). The couple generally does not remove their clothes, but simply rearranges them enough to allow for access and intercourse. The man then stands behind the woman and enters her from behind.

436 Try the woman flying position. In this position, the man stands behind the woman, and she leans forward onto a chair or the edge of the bed. The man stands between her legs, lifts her legs, and enters her, while holding the lower half of her body up in the air.

437 TRY THE THREADED NEEDLE POSITION. The man lies down on his back, bringing his knees up toward his chest. The woman gets in between his legs, and guides him into her. The man may need to lift his pelvis (or prop it up on pillows) to help this along.

438 PLOW THE FIELD. In this position, the woman props her legs up by resting them on a chair or the edge of the bed. Facing the floor, she supports herself with her hands planted on the floor. The man straddles her, and enters her from behind (and above).

439 HAVE SEX IN FRONT OF A MIRROR. Okay, technically, this isn't a position in and of itself. But it is a move that increases the pleasure you can get out of all the other positions. Men, especially, tend to be visual creatures and can get really turned on by watching themselves having sex with their partners.

440 ADD MORE MIRRORS. It just makes sense that if one mirror is exciting, several more mirrors would be many times better. Try having sex in front of several strategically placed mirrors. This arrangement will allow you to see yourself (and your partner) from all sorts of interesting angles.

441 TRY FURNITURE SPECIALLY DESIGNED FOR INTERESTING POSITIONS. Again, this tip isn't exactly a position, but it's a way to come up with all kinds of new and exciting positions. Check out some of the "lovers' furniture" designed specifically for sex play. The most common type of furniture is an item that can be flipped or rearranged into several different shapes or configurations: a wedge-shaped incline, a set of steps, and so on. Look for these online or at larger adult toy stores.

CHAPTER 10

ORGASMS

Orgasms are often seen as the "main event" of a sexual experience. In reality, it's possible to have a satisfying sexual and romantic encounter without an orgasm. In fact, many ancient peoples believed that males should avoid having an orgasm because it supposedly drained him of vital life energy.

However, times have changed and modern couples value—and oftentimes seem to obsess over—the orgasm. Orgasms provide an emotional release in addition to the physical climax. Many people find orgasms to be a deeply emotional experience. There is also the ego factor. Many people judge their own performance based on whether or not they are able to give their partner an orgasm. Orgasm (specifically male orgasm) can also be desirable from a practical standpoint—such as when the couple is trying to conceive. Bottom line: Orgasms are important to a lot of people. With that in mind, here are orgasm-related things for you to try.

442 **HAVE AN ORGASM.** Okay, start simple. Just try to have one plain, old ordinary orgasm. With luck, that is no big challenge for you, but some people do have difficulty—in which case, trying a few of the other moves in this book may be helpful. ♥

443 **GO FOR MORE THAN ONE.** If you have successfully had one simple orgasm without any trouble, you might need more of a challenge to make things exciting. Now, try to have more than one orgasm within a short time frame. (You can do this yourself or with your partner.) ♥♥

444 **TRY TO MASTER THE ART OF ACHIEVING MULTIPLE ORGASMS.** Okay, I will assume you have achieved one orgasm—and even two—without a problem. Now up the ante and try to have several (more than two) orgasms in a short time frame. Again, it is up to you whether to do this alone or with your partner. ♥♥

445 **TIME YOUR RECOVERY PERIOD.** This is the time you need in order to recover after having one orgasm before you can have another. Women are often able to have multiple orgasms with short recovery periods in between, whereas men tend to need a bit longer to recover between climaxes. ♥

446 **TRY TO SET NEW PERSONAL BEST RECOVERY PERIOD RECORD.** Keep track of your recovery

period times. See how quickly you can have two (or more) orgasms in a row. Try out a few of your own unique techniques to improve your time. Figure out if there are factors (such as time of day) that seem to affect your recovery time.   ♥♥

447 **MAKE IT A HABIT TO HAVE MULTIPLE ORGASMS.** See if you can have multiple orgasms on a regular basis. You do not necessarily need to force yourself to have multiple orgasms every single time you have sex—but it's nice to do it as much as you can (or as much as you want to).   ♥♥

448 **TRY A DRY ORGASM.** Men: see if you can master the popular Tantra technique of "dry orgasms," or orgasms without ejaculation. They are supposed to allow people to benefit from the release of an orgasm without the "grand finale" aspect that is often connected with ejaculation. (Many ancient peoples believed ejaculation drained a man of a valuable life force.)   ♥

449 **DON'T COME JUST YET, IF YOU CAN AVOID IT.** Prolong your orgasm for as long as you can. This is especially important for men, if you are the type of guy who calls it quits as soon as you climax. Enlist your partner's help in devising some strategies to help you stall your climax as long as possible.   ♥♥

450 **PRACTICE THE STOP-START TECHNIQUE.** This is a technique men often use in order to last as long as possible before orgasm. Go along with sex as you normally would. Then, when you near the point of climax, stop all sexual activity. Don't even let your partner touch you. Wait for the urge to subside, then start up again. Do this as many times as you can (or as long as you wish).

451 PROLONG ORGASM. If you often reach your climax (and then want to go to sleep) before your partner, you need to come up with ways to maximize your "staying power." Do some research—there are plenty of tricks that are recommended for helping to stall your orgasm.

452 TRY TO REACH ORGASM WITHOUT TOUCHING. See if you can manage to have an orgasm without any direct physical stimulation at all. Watching porn is allowed, as is fantasizing. Some people claim to be able to do this, while other people find it impossible.

453 MAKE IT QUICK—ON PURPOSE. Men: We have all heard those unflattering stories about the "two-minute man." Just for fun, see how closely you can come to hitting that mark. This is one time when you are allowed (encouraged, even) to be quick. Your partner can help if she likes.

454 TRY TO HIT THE TWO-MINUTE MARK. Once you have had a few "quick, on purpose" experiences, make it a game with your partner. Start timing from the second she first touches you, and see if she can get you to climax at exactly the two-minute point. ♥

455 CAN SHE BE A TWO-MINUTE WOMAN? Guys, now it is your turn to return the favor and see how quickly you can help your partner reach a climax. It usually takes women longer to climax, so you do not necessarily need to try to hit the two-minute mark. Just focus on helping her set a new personal record. ♥♥

456 COME TOGETHER. Try to achieve orgasm simultaneously with your partner. Make it a game, and keep it fun. Putting too much pressure on the timing can make it difficult for your partner to relax. Guys, you may need to employ some stalling techniques to give your partner a chance to catch up to you. ♥♥♥

457 FIGURE OUT SOME FAIL-SAFE TECHNIQUES. See if you and your partner can devise a routine in which you can almost be sure to climax simultaneously (or nearly so) on a regular basis. It may take a while for the two of your to learn each other's routine and timetable. ♥♥

458 GIVE HIM A "BI-GASM." This occurs by stimulating two major erogenous zones simultaneously. Dr. Cadell offers these tips: "You can stimulate his penis with your hands while stimulating his testicles with your mouth. You can also sit on his penis while stimulating his prostate. See how many other variations you can come up with to enable your lover to have a bi-gasm and he'll think you are a sexpert!"

459 GIVE HER A "BI-GASM." Stimulate at least two of her hot zones simultaneously, and see if you can give her a double orgasm.

460 TRY TO CLIMAX VIA PROSTATE STIMULATION. Men: See if you can achieve an orgasm via your partner stimulating your prostate gland (in other words, anal stimulation). Some men enjoy this, although many men are squeamish at even the thought of any kind of anal stimulation.

461 GIVE HIM A FULL-BODY ORGASM. Many people believe a man can have a "full-body" orgasm. This involves an orgasm of the "male g-spot" (the prostate) as well as a "regular" orgasm. To help him achieve a full-body orgasm, stimulate him anally (with your hand or a sex toy) while also bringing him to a climax as you normally would. This may take some practice, but that's half the fun.

462 CLIMAX THROUGH CLITORAL STIMULATION. Women: See how long it actually takes you to achieve an orgasm via direct clitoral stimulation (either by yourself or with your partner, using either his hands or mouth). For most women, this is the easiest way to reach an orgasm.

463 **CLIMAX MORE QUICKLY THROUGH CLITORAL STIMULATION.** Women, now that you are experienced at reaching orgasm via direct clitoral stimulation, try to set a new record. Test out a few different techniques (such as using different types of toys) to see what helps you reach that point the fastest. 💗💗

464 **SEE IF YOU CAN CLIMAX WITHOUT CLITORAL STIMULATION.** Women: See how long it takes you to have an orgasm without clitoral stimulation. You (or your partner) can use vaginal stimulation or other physical contact. Most women say trying to achieve orgasm without involving stimulation of the clitoris is more difficult. 💗

465 **LOCATE YOUR OWN G-SPOT.** Women: see if you can find your g-spot, if you do not already know where it is. (Hint: It is a small area in the upper wall of the vagina, about one to two inches from the opening.) It may be sensitive to direct pressure. 💗

466 **LOCATE YOUR PARTNER'S G-SPOT.** Men: try to find your partner's g-spot. She can help guide the way if she already knows where it is. If not, the two of you can do some research online beforehand to get some clues as to where to find it. 💗💗

467 **HAVE A G-SPOT CLIMAX.** Women: try to have a g-spot orgasm (also sometimes called a "vaginal orgasm"). According to reports from women who have

experienced these, they feel much different than a clitoral orgasm. Let your partner help (he will love helping you explore new territory).

468 **ORGASM ON YOUR PARTNER'S BODY.** This is mainly something men would do. To avoid any unpleasant scenes, get your partner's okay beforehand, if possible. Watching yourself climax on your partner's breasts, belly, face, or other body parts can be very exciting, especially if she seems to enjoy it.

469 **LET YOUR PARTNER CLIMAX ON YOUR BODY.** Ladies, this is mainly directed toward you. There is a reason why the "money shot" is a staple of all porn movies. Men really get off on seeing their juices spurting all over their partner. Sure, it's kind of hardcore and dirty and may not look very pretty, but it is highly arousing for them. To lessen the chance of any unpleasant surprises, try to discuss this beforehand. Let them know which parts of your body are okay (and not okay) for climax "landing zones."

470 **TRY TO ACHIEVE (OR INCREASE) FEMALE EJACULATION.** Women do release a burst of fluids upon orgasm, but it is generally not as heavy or noticeable as that of a man's. However, some women do release a stream of female ejaculation fluids—in some cases, enough that it squirts out of her with force. There are women who claim this is an art, a technique that can be learned. That's debatable, but it might be interesting to give it a try. Do some research, and try to practice a few "female ejaculate" techniques. See if you notice any difference.

471 BRING HER TO ORGASM USING A TOY. Yes, we know you want to get in there and get a piece of the action yourself. Be patient, your time will come. Right now, this is her time. Try to bring her to orgasm solely by pleasuring her with a sex toy.

472 BRING HIM TO ORGASM USING A SEX TOY. This may be a bit tougher, simply because there are fewer sex toys for men. Ladies, use your shopping skills to find the perfect toy. Cock rings and fake vaginas and/or fake mouths are usually good choices.

473 GIVE YOUR PARTNER THE NIGHT OFF. Many people feel like they cannot wrap up the sexual encounter until their partner has climaxed. This is especially true for men, who will often try to prolong their own orgasm until after their partner has achieved hers. Tonight, let your partner off the hook. Tell him you don't need an orgasm (or you will take care if it yourself later), so he is free to just concentrate on his own satisfaction.

474 PUSH ON HIS PERINEUM (GENTLY). Just as your man is about to climax, gently push on his perineum (the area between his testicles and anus). Many men claim this intensifies their orgasms. Keep in mind, this is a very sensitive area, so approach it gingerly and stop at the first sign of any discomfort on his part. ♥♥♥

475 **FAKE AN ORGASM.** Whether you tell your partner is up to you. If you have already had to do this at some point (or several), it will be no big deal. If you have never faked an orgasm, consider yourself lucky. This is your chance to give it a try. ♥

476 **ADMIT IT IF YOU DIDN'T HAVE AN ORGASM.** Except for the one experiment in #475, if you do not have an orgasm, don't fake it. Just come clean and admit it to your partner. Warning: Being honest could result in hurting your partner's feelings and/or an uncomfortable conversation in which you analyze the whole situation. ♥

CHAPTER 11

ACTIVITIES YOU CAN SHARE

Sharing a fun activity together can be a great way to strengthen your romantic bond and help the two of you to feel closer to each other. It really doesn't even matter what the particular activity is. Just spending quality time together and having a good time is all that matters. Not only will you create special memories, you also show each other that spending time on your relationship is a top priority. And if you can create a romantic mood as a result of your shared experience, you are much more likely to want to make love when you get home (if you can even wait that long). If your shared activity involves any kind of physical exertion, even better—the endorphins will give your libido a little extra kick.

477 **SHARE SOME ART APPRECIATION.** Go to a museum and check out the erotic art and nudes. If you like to draw, bring along a sketchpad and sketch a sexy or nude portrait of your partner. You will have to rely on memory for the nude part, as the museum will probably call security if you get naked in the middle of the gallery. Find a quiet, secluded area to do a little romantic petting and kissing.

478 **BET YOU'LL HAVE FUN WITH THIS ONE.** Go out for an afternoon of horses and bets; horseracing is always more fun when you've got $2 to win on the nose of the long shot. Only bet on horses whose names can have some kind of naughty connotation (see how creative you can be in coming up with the double-entendres). Make a side bet as to who wins the most.

479 **ATTEND A BURLESQUE SHOW.** Watch the beautiful dancers go through their sexy and sensual moves (ladies, pay attention and see if you can learn a few moves). Generally, these dancers don't get totally nude, so there is an element of mystery there—and it might be less intimidating for women to watch than a totally nude strip show.

480 **SIT THROUGH A CHICK FLICK.** Guys, even if you can barely stand it, take her to the latest romantic comedy or drama. Kiss her on the neck so she doesn't miss any of the action. It may just put her in the mood for

some action herself! If you like, you can offer to act out some of the romantic scenes with her when the two of you get home.

481 ATTEND A TANTRIC SEX WORKSHOP WITH YOUR PARTNER. These can range from mild to wild. Some involve nudity and interaction with your partner (or perhaps an instructor or another person). It can be very exciting—and educational. Just be sure you're clear on exactly what will happen at the workshop beforehand.

482 ADD SOME MOUSSE TO YOUR LOVEMAKING. Hit the bedroom and have fun trying out the latest in personal lubricants. Intimate mousses are the latest rage. The ones made by Replens come in flavors like cinnamon and vanilla, don't stain the sheets, and won't leave a messy sticky residue.

483 FIND OUT WHY GETTING SMART (TOGETHER) CAN BE SEXY, TOO. Broaden your minds together. Enroll in a college class (even just a short community course) together in something that interests both of you. Massage is an ideal one but any course can be romantic if you take the right approach. What about learning French?

484 WATCH YOUR PARTNER'S FAVORITE TV SHOW TOGETHER—WITH A SEXY TWIST. Sit cuddled with your partner through his favorite TV show and let him explain everything about it. Do this (with a smile) even if you hate science fiction or whatever he likes. Add a sexy twist by removing a piece of clothing during each commercial break or engaging in foreplay whenever the plot begins to get slow.

485 **BE SPORTY TOGETHER—BUT MAKE IT SEXY AND HOT.** Try a new sport together. All that sweating and rising endorphins are sure to make you contemplate other physical activities. But to up the stakes, figure out a way to add an erotic element. First, wear as little clothing as possible—or at least wear something tight. Then, add lots of physical contact and place a wager, with a sex-related reward for the winner.

486 **SEE THE STARS.** Read a few astronomy websites and watch for details of full moons, blue moons, eclipses, and meteor showers. Then head out to watch nature's display. You will be in awe, and it will be the ultimate romantic setting for a perfect late-night romp under the stars.

487 **GRANT WISHES.** Give your partner an "As You Wish Day." Let her direct your actions for the day and say yes to whatever she requests. (Here is a little secret: Chances are, some of her wishes will probably be things you secretly would wish for, too.)

488 **LOOK INTO THE FUTURE.** Have some fun with your local fortuneteller and find out what awaits you in the future. Go into it with an "anything goes" approach, and have your palms or cards read. Ask the fortuneteller to specifically focus on your sex life. Keep in mind that no matter what the outcome, your future together is what you make of it. ♥

489 SHOPPING CAN BE A SPORT. For a great challenge, head to your local mall for a shopping spree with a twist. Pick your limit and spend exactly one hour trying to find the perfect gift for your significant other. Meet in the food court and decide who did a better job. ♥

490 PUMP IT UP—IN THE NUDE (OR NEARLY NUDE). A good workout can be the best aphrodisiac because it releases endorphins and gets blood flowing to all those sensitive parts. But you can make it extra sexy by wearing no clothing (or very little clothing). When you're done working out, you can hit the shower together. ♥♥

491 IT'S OFFICIAL—YOU'RE A PICTURE PERFECT COUPLE. Arrange for a couples glamour portrait for posterity. Enjoy the pampering. Come up with as many romantic poses as you can. Get a large print to hang in a prominent place in your house where you will see it every day. ♥

492 GET SOME PRIVATE PICS JUST FOR YOUR PARTNER. This is a sexier version of the photo shoot idea: Get some nude (or at least as sexy as possible) pictures of yourself taken on your own, and then present them to your partner as a surprise when the two of you are alone.

493 DO A "HIGH EXPOSURE" PHOTO SESSION. Here is an even sexier version: Do a nude photo shoot together with a professional photographer. Each of you can keep a small wallet-sized picture with you all the time, and look it at whenever you like.

494 TAKE TURNS PLAYING PHOTOGRAPHER. If you don't want to have a stranger taking your sexy shots, take them yourselves. Take turns being the shutterbug and putting each other into sexy poses. Or, set the autotimer and work sexy poses together.

495 LET HIM GIVE YOU A RIDE, LITERALLY. If possible, try to carpool to work together, at least once in a while. Talking about your workday adds a charming emotional dimension to your relationship. Encouragement from your partner will translate to higher confidence at work. If possible, stop off for a quickie in a secluded spot, or at least do a little bit of making out. You will arrive at the office in a good mood and ready to face the day.

496 ENJOY SOME HORSE-AND-BUGGY HIJINKS. Spontaneously jump into a horse-drawn carriage, cuddle under the blanket, and watch the rest of the tourists who are eyeing you enviously. Let them wonder what the two of you are doing under that blanket. Ask the driver (or a passerby) to snap your picture as a memento of this romantic occasion. 🖤🖤

497 TAKE A HOTEL HIDEAWAY. Share a getaway with your partner in which you go nowhere special; any big hotel chain with a pool and room service will do. Leave the Blackberry home; set the cell phone to voicemail. Give yourself permission to do as much (or as little) as you want. 🖤🖤

498 ENJOY A ROMANTIC COUPLES-ONLY WEEK-END. Plan a weekend or a week at a couples-only destination. For cheesy fun, try the Pocono Mountains in Pennsylvania, with its heart-shaped individual baths. Make friends with all the honeymooners, and pretend you two are honeymooners as well. 🖤🖤

499 TRY A RACIER COUPLES-ONLY GETAWAY. For a more erotic affair, with "clothing optional" standards, try Hedonism in Jamaica. Be prepared to shed your inhibitions. Don't worry about what anyone will think—nobody knows who you are, so you are free to be as wild as you want. 🖤🖤🖤

500 HAVE A REALLY RACY COUPLES-ONLY GET-AWAY. Head to a swingers' retreat. Even if you don't join in the activities, seeing all the sex going on around you is sure to give you a few ideas of how to keep your partner happy during the trip. 🖤🖤🖤🖤

501 **HAVE A "NOTHING IS OFF-LIMITS" GETAWAY.** Before you and your partner head off on your racy getaway, one or both of you must vow to do anything your partner (or anyone else) dares or coerces you into doing. This is not for the wimpy or squeamish.

502 **GET EROTIC IN THE OCEAN.** Take classes together in something fun and wet, such as windsurfing, surfing, or scuba diving. And if you have to travel to get there, all the better. Once your lessons are over, find something else to do together in the ocean.

503 **MUD AND SWEAT CAN BE SEXY.** Play a game of mud football with your partner. Tackling is optional, but you can put a sexy spin on the term "touch football." Then you can do a little mud wrestling, or have fun hosing each other down.

504 **MAKE KARAOKE NIGHT AS KINKY AS YOU CAN.** When you and your partner are out with your friends, share a private insider erotic secret. Make a deal in advance that specific songs will signify specific sex act you will perform when you get home. Keep your partner in anticipation of which song you will pick. Then make your performance as sexy as possible.

505 **BE SEXY LIKE BOGEY AND BACALL.** There's something to be said for the timeless classic sexiness portrayed by old Hollywood. Cleo, of Cleo's Boutique (*www.cleosboutique.com*) gives this suggestion: Dress up in your best Bacall and Bogart (or Cary Grant) attire and head for the most glamorous hotel lobby in town. Flirt outrageously while nursing your martini, until you absolutely must leave. Together. End the evening as you imagine the Hollywood legends would.

506 ACT LIKE HOT HONEYMOONERS. Rent a convertible, drive to a nearby B&B for the weekend, and tell people that you are on your honeymoon, even if you're not. If you prefer heading to the city, splurge on the honeymoon suite at a luxury hotel.

507 ENJOY THE PRIVACY OF A PRIVATE PLANE. Hire a limousine to take you to the local airport, where you have arranged for a ride into the setting sun in a small plane. Feel free to get romantic while you're up in the air.

508 RIDE THE RAILS. Take an extended passenger train trip. Pack very nice attire, and travel as if you're Cary Grant and Eva Marie Saint in *North by Northwest*. For extra fun, each of you must stick to a persona you've created ahead of time. Don't tell your partner anything about the persona, let it come out over the course of the trip. Dress for dinner, and have mysterious conversations, and flirt with each other. Excuse yourselves from the table separately, and make the other diners wonder if you're complete strangers or secret lovers.

509 **HAVE A ROMANTIC PLAY DATE.** Arrange with her boss to get her an afternoon off, and pick her up from work. Drive into the city, and go to the observation deck of one of the tall buildings. While she's still mystified as to what the trip is all about, tell her you just wanted to say you love her in a memorable way. Give her a special gift, such as a piece of jewelry, with the date engraved on it. Have someone take your picture, and put it in an engraved frame.

510 **TRY A MASSAGE THAT WILL RUB YOU BOTH THE RIGHT WAY.** Get a couple's massage in a romantic setting. Use your imagination. Atop a romantic hotel rooftop, an afternoon couple's massage can set the mood for a passionate evening. You will be loosened up and stress-free (and possibly still covered in oil).

511 **ADD SOME WINE TO YOUR ROMANCE.** Go on a wine tour with your partner. A scenic wine tasting at a picturesque chateau in the romantic countryside will instantly whisk you and your partner off to a charming world where nothing else exists but the two of you.

512 **HIT THE ROAD.** Take a road trip with your partner when you have no planned destination. Be ready for anything. Stop whenever and wherever the mood strikes. The possibilities are endless on the open road. Make the most of this exciting adventure.

513 DISCOVER WHY PIT STOPS CAN BE A PLEA-
SURE. While the two of you are on your road trip, look
for the most romantic place you can find and pull over
for a quickie. Be sure to put a star on the map for every
place you've had a sexual encounter along the way.

514 MAKE YOUR OWN BEAUTIFUL SCENERY. Here
is a different twist: Look for the most unromantic
places you can find, and challenge yourselves to figure out a way to have a hot encounter there, despite
the lackluster environment. Beauty is in the eye of the
beholder, after all.

515 CREATE A PRIVATE ESCAPE CLAUSE. Create
a secret code word for the next time you're both at a
party or conversation that you wish to escape—and get
busy! This will keep you both excited and give you the
chance to exchange knowing smiles for the remainder
of the night.

516 MAKE YOUR OWN SEX TOYS. This is one do-it-
yourself project you will really enjoy doing together.
There are lots of ways to make your own sex toys: You
can gather up feathers to make your own tickler, decorate some scarves or blindfolds with your own special touches—or even make your own ice dildo (which
provides an amazing sensation—do an online search
for instructions or to order a mold).

517 **H**AVE A MIDWEEK RENDEZVOUS. Book a hotel room midweek in the city (maybe even during your lunch hour). It is cheap but guaranteed to add some spice—and may even cut down on your commute time the next day if you do stay overnight.

518 **P**UT THE "CHILD" BACK IN WILD CHILD. Be a kid again, and head for a weekend at a resort that has an indoor water park. Or, hit the sledding hill and experience the thrill of racing down on a toboggan at breakneck speed squeezing each other tightly and laughing and screaming. Remember the hot cocoa for warming up in the car!

519 **T**OUR A NUDIST COLONY. Dana Barish says, "Most nudist resorts allow visitors but only if you shed all your clothes when you get to the front entrance. How hot would it be to walk around in the buff with your partner talking to many strangers who are also naked? You probably won't make it down the road without having to pull over for some steamy sex thanks to being riled up all day."

520 **H**AVE SEX IN THE COLD. Really cold—as cold as you can stand it. This can be done either outside in the winter, or indoors if you turn the heat off and let it get really chilly. You'll be forced to snuggle together, and will appreciate the body heat. And the cold air against your bare skin will send chills (literally) through your body.

521 $\mathcal{H}$AVE SEX IN A SINGLE BED. Meaning, those small beds designed for one person. The tight quarters will force you to get really close and come up with all kinds of new positions. Plus, you'll feel like naughty teenagers (or like college kids trying not to wake up your room-mates).

522 $\mathcal{D}$ESIGNATE A SPECIAL—AND UNIQUE—SEX SPOT. Nothing says you two are a couple like having your own "special spot." Have something specific on or near your property that is only for the two of you to enjoy during intimate encounters, such as a hammock or a two-person pool float. Never let anyone else use it. No exceptions.

523 $\mathcal{M}$AKE YOUR OWN THRILLS ON THE THRILL RIDES. Go on a date at an amusement park. Get romantic and/or intimate on as many different rides as possible. Be creative. Oh, and figure out a way to do it without shocking any nearby children (or their disap-proving parents).

CHAPTER 12

FUN AND GAMES

To keep the passion alive in your relationship, it's important to have fun—in and out of the bedroom. Games can keep you laughing while strengthening your bond—and anything that puts you in a good mood always has the potential to lead to more intimate fun.

Obviously, adult or X-rated games are great for couples to use as foreplay. And there are plenty of those kinds of games out there. But don't limit yourself to strictly adult games. Be creative. Take some mainstream games and figure out a way to put a naughty spin on them. With a little ingenuity, even the tamest of games can be "sexed up" to make for erotic fun. Chances are, you have plenty of games in your house right now that would work very well.

524 PLAY TWISTER TOGETHER. This game is a favorite among teenagers and college kids. When you and your partner are twisted into interesting positions, you're sure to get some ideas of what else the two of you can do together. Clothing is optional.

525 PLAY A ROUND OF "NAUGHTY SCRABBLE." Make up some adults-only rules. Some ideas: all words must be X-rated, or they must be words you can some- how work into a sexy sentence. You can give bonus points for words that are extra hot.

526 ENJOY A ROLE-PLAYING GAME. Role-play your favorite fantasies with a deck of fantasy cards, like those available at *www.fantasyplayingcards.com*.

527 PLAY A GAME OF HOT CHESS. For every piece that is taken, the person doing the taking gets two or three minutes of the sexy treat of his or her choice. Have a kitchen timer on hand to keep the game moving (hopefully toward the bedroom!).

528 TRY A GAME OF "KISSING OTHELLO." Again, be creative in making up your own sexy rules. An exam- ple: You earn one kiss for every flip you make—a kiss you can plant wherever you decide on your partner. This just might make it worth losing!

529 MAKE UP A BOOK OF "CARNAL COUPONS" FOR YOUR PARTNER. Create a book of coupons, each of which entitles the bearer to a specific sexy treat. Some examples: a sensual massage, an extended session of oral sex, a quickie, etc. Your partner will get a thrill each time he or she redeems one of these coupons.

530 **H**AVE A COSTUME DAY. Rent some funny or thematic costumes for a day, and just wear them together, all day. The costumes can just be silly, or they can be sexy to make this game even hotter. Act as though it's perfectly normal to do this.

531 **C**REATE YOUR OWN LANGUAGE. This is a great game to play at cocktail parties. Before you arrive, agree on certain phrases to use that only the two of you will understand. For example, "That is fascinating" means "This person is so boring" or "I'll have to try that" means "Let's get out of here." The private joke will be a secret for only the two of you to enjoy.

532 **C**REATE YOUR OWN NAUGHTY LANGUAGE. Figure out your own special terms or words that only the two of you understand. This way, you can exchange dirty comments in public and nobody will know. Example: "The weather has been unseasonably warm" could actually mean, "I'm getting wet just thinking about what we will do later."

533 **E**XCHANGE ADULT GOODIE BASKETS. Set aside a time when you and your partner will each create special "Lovers Only" baskets for each other. Establish a spending and a time limit only, but not too many other restrictions. Exchange at the same time, and take turns enjoying your treats together.

534 **T**RY THE EROTIC ALPHABET GAME. Go through the alphabet and try to think of a body part that starts with each letter. Then you can take turns on the letters, kissing the body part that begins with that letter for at least thirty seconds. You may never get to Z.

535 **P**LAY STRIP POKER WITH YOUR PARTNER. Strip poker is one of those classic adult games that every-body has heard about, but few people have actually played. This sexy game can bring a whole new mean-ing to the phrase, "All in." Not to mention, "I've got the nuts."

536 **P**LAY STRIP POKER WITH YOUR PARTNER— AND OTHER PEOPLE. This takes a lot more nerve. You need to choose your poker partners wisely. Make sure they are people you know very well (or, perhaps, people you would like to get to know very well).

537 **H**AVE A STRIP POKER DINNER. Dr. Cadell says, "The best way to play strip poker is to surprise your lover by playing the game while dinner is in the oven. Once the game is underway, be prepared to lose one article of clothing with each hand that you lose. Everybody wins when you're both naked and the mood changes from competitive to sexy. Make sure you serve and eat dinner in the nude to top off the evening."

♥♥♥

538 **PLAY DIRTY POOL.** Take turns shooting, and the person not shooting needs to do anything sexy to distract the shooter. Scratches lose a piece of clothing. The person who sinks the eight ball too soon and/or loses also must forfeit a piece of clothing. Can you guess what will be happening on the table at the end? ♥♥

539 **PLAY TRUTH OR DARE WITH YOUR PART-NER.** This is an oldie but goodie. Make the questions or dares as racy as you like. You can play this alone with your partner—or, if you are really brave, play it with a group of friends (preferably other couples). Following are some suggestions to get you started. ♥♥

540 **TRUTH IDEAS #1.** What's the one sex trick you've always wanted to try, but never had the nerve? Have you ever realized someone was watching you have sex—and you kind of liked it? What would you most like me to do to you right now? ♥♥

541 **TRUTH IDEAS #2.** What would you really think about having a threesome? If you could be the opposite sex for a day, what sex act(s) would you most want to do? What public place would you be willing to have sex in/at? What is your secret turn-on? ♥♥

542 **T**RUTH IDEAS #**3.** What's the longest you have ever gone without masturbating? What's the strangest thing you have ever used as a makeshift sex toy? What really dirty word gets you hot? Do you like to be spanked—and, if so, how hard? Have you ever looked at porn at work?

543 **T**RUTH IDEAS #**4.** Have you ever "earned" a back-stage pass? Have you ever been "paid" (either with cash or expensive merchandise) to have sex? Have you ever paid for sex? What was your most embarrassing sexual experience? Has anyone ever caught you when you were in the middle of having sex?

544 **D**ARE IDEAS #1 (FOR A MAN TO DARE A WOMAN). I dare you to kiss (insert name of your partner's hot female friend). I dare you to lick whipped cream off (body part of yourself or your partner). I dare you to show me how you masturbated the last time you did it.

545 **D**ARE IDEA #2 (FOR A MAN TO DARE A WOMAN). I dare you to let me come in your mouth (or you can substitute another body part). Obviously, this is something you would want to discuss—and then act out—with your partner when the two of you are alone.

546 **D**ARE IDEA #3 (FOR A WOMAN TO DARE MAN). I dare you to try an anal plug (or let me stimulate you anally). Again, this is something to discuss and act out privately. Be warned, ladies: Once you open the door by suggesting this dare, your partner is likely to turn the table and dare you to do the same thing when it's his turn.

547 DARE IDEAS #4. I dare you to say something dirty in front of (insert name of someone you both know, preferably someone who is easily shocked). I dare you to stand naked (or topless) in front of the window. I dare you to let me blindfold you for ten minutes while I do whatever I want to you.

548 DARE IDEAS #5. I dare you to go a week without masturbating (a.k.a., the Seinfeld dare). I dare you to "accidentally" flash someone when we go out in public tonight. I dare you to let me spank you. I dare you to let me spank your bare ass. I dare you to spank me—hard.

549 DARE IDEAS #6. I dare you to dress up like a cheerleader or athlete. I dare you to dress up like a hooker or pimp. I dare you to pinch a stranger's ass in public. I dare you to use (insert name of sex toy of choice), or let me use it on you.

550 CREATE YOUR OWN DECK OF SEX CARDS. On each card, list a position, sex act, accessory, or other sexy element. Illustrate each with a drawing or picture (print them out from the web or cut them out of adult mags). This can work in a variety of ways: Shuffle the deck and pick a few at random, or take turns creating your own perfect "winning hand."

551 PLAY A SEXY MEMORY GAME. Tell your partner a short story from your past, or a few fun facts about yourself. Then quiz them by asking a few questions related to what you just told them. Reward them for each right answer by removing an article of clothing or providing a special romantic treat. This promotes communication and listening skills while also leading to a sexy encounter.

552 PLAY THE "I ONCE THOUGHT ABOUT DOING . . ." GAME. Take turns where you and your partner each reveal something sexual that you once thought about, imagined, or otherwise envisioned. This allows you to throw something out there for discussion or consideration in a safe way that doesn't leave you feeling quite so vulnerable.

553 HAVE FUN WITH THE HOSE. The garden hose, that is. If you pick a warm night (and your yard is relatively secluded) you can enjoy some erotic water play with the hose (or even the sprinkler). One downside: Generally, the water tends to be pretty chilly.

554 PLAY "MAY I KISS YOU THERE?" Sitting on the couch, take your partner by the hand and ask, "May I kiss your hand?" She'll catch on pretty quick, don't worry. Follow with the forearm, the elbow, the shoulder, the clavicle, each side of the neck, the eyelids, and the earlobe ... make it as fun and sexy as you can imagine. Save the mouth for when you're both naked and there is nothing left to kiss!

555 HAVE A WATER FIGHT. Start a water fight on a hot summer day. Sneak up on your partner with the hose, and let them try to wrestle it away from you. When you give up, plant a wet kiss on their lips, and suggest going inside and getting out of those wet clothes.

556 GO ROCK CLIMBING. Try rock climbing together at your local gym. With a rock climbing gym in most major cities, this fun activity is sure to enliven the spirits of any couple. Nothing establishes trust like a belay lesson and a journey up a 30-foot rock wall. Not to mention, the adrenaline rush will release lots of endorphins that may give your libido a kickstart.

557 TEASE YOUR PARTNER. Have your partner lay naked and blindfolded on the bed. Tell her not to move or talk—if she does, gently remind her, "ah—ah— no talking." Have a basket of interesting items handy to tickle her skin with—a feather, string, a soft-petaled thornless flower. Then try more daring things like chocolate pudding—if she can't smell it, you can use your hot tongue to lick the cold pudding off. Tell your partner she must guess what each item is before moving on to the next, or she won't win the prize (which is you!).

558 HAVE GOODIE NIGHT. Each of you buy a good selection of various fun adult goodies, and make one night of the week the "goodie night." Wrap a big box in fun paper to make it a festive occasion, and cut a hole in the top so you can fish around for what feels interesting. Leave everything in its original packaging, if you can, so it's harder to tell what you're choosing.

559 PLAY "EVERYTHING BUT." Have a game of "everything but . . ." and see how long you can stand not doing it. The one who lasts the longest without begging for it is the winner! Keep track with a tally sheet, and you can taunt each other about who has more willpower.

560 MANLY MICROPHONE. Walk up naked behind your wife while she's busy working at a table or desk. Ask her what she's doing. After she responds, say, "I didn't hear you, could you speak into the microphone?" When she turns around, if it isn't a turn-on, it should at least be good for a laugh.

561 SWAP SECRET FANTASIES. Each of you writes down what fantasy you would want your partner to fulfill, and put them in two containers. Each draws one out of the other's container in the morning before work, but doesn't reveal which one. The anticipation will have all day to build!

562 STOCK UP ON ADULT GAMES. Buy some adult board games. They can be a great way to help you break the ice in the bedroom without doing anything too scary. Plus, you can't be blamed for anything you might suggest. Hey, it's not like it was your idea (wink, wink)—it's the game's fault! You are simply following the rules. The best part: there really are no losers with these games. Everyone ends up feeling like a winner!

563 TRY SOME OF THESE SEXY GAMES. They're available at many online game sites (such as *www.boardgames .com*) and adult retailers. The Kama Sutra Game—have fun while building the intimacy in your relationship. Would You Rather?—this game, which is available in DVD format, is designed to encourage you to open up and reveal some of your secrets.

564 TRY MORE OF THESE EROTIC GAMES. Romantic Sensations game—sets the scene for a sexy and romantic experience by encouraging you to explore your senses. The game includes massage lotion and bath gel. Advanced Sex Techniques game—provides more than 100,000 sex adventure combinations. Lust!—the game cards instruct you to act out various romantic and sexual pleasures with your partner.

565 MIX-AND-MATCH BODY ACTION GAME. Each person writes down ten body parts on separate index cards and puts them in a pile. Then each person writes down a sexy action to perform, such as kissing, licking, massaging, etc. Shuffle each pile separately, and decide who gets to go first. The player turns over one card from each pile and then performs the sexy action on that body part. You may not make it through all the cards, but they're reusable for round two! 🖤🖤🖤

566 MAKE A "SEXY SUGGESTIONS" BOX. It takes the basic boring suggestion box and makes it much hotter. Each of you can jot down various sex moves or adventures you'd like to try, listing each one on a separate piece of paper (one color for him, another color for her). When the mood strikes, pluck one of your partner's suggestions from the box—and make the wish come true. 🖤🖤🖤

567 PLAY CARNIVAL GAMES WITH A SEXY TWIST. Who says these games are just for kids? To make your next trip to the carnival more fun, make a deal with your partner by adding some exciting stakes. Agree that whoever wins the most prizes gets to be the boss in the bedroom that night. 🖤🖤

568 BUY MORE ADULT GAMES. If you have already played (and gotten bored with) the same old adult board games, add some exciting new games to your collection. Visit a website such as *www.areyougame.com* and you and your partner can pick out a certain number of games each. 🖤🖤

569 MAKE UP YOUR OWN GAMES. Nobody says you have to limit yourself to the adult games already available in stores. If you can come up with something better, go for it. Feel free to use props and come up with creative prizes (or punishments for whoever loses).

570 **CREATE A KINKY SCAVENGER HUNT.** This is a fun game to play with your partner. Put some thought into the items you will include on your list. The twist: Instead of just finding the items, you or your partner must then use them in some erotic way.

571 **CREATE YOUR OWN UNIQUE NAMES FOR YOUR FAVORITE SEX ACTS.** Be as silly or creative as you like. Take turns deciding who gets to create the next name. It will be like an inside joke when you and your partner refer to, say, the "Purple Butterfly" in public.

572 **CHALLENGE YOUR PARTNER TO CREATE ACTS TO FIT YOUR NICKNAMES.** Come up with some funny or original nicknames or phrases—say, "The General's Salute." Now, challenge your partner to try and come up with some sex position or erotic act that would be a good fit for that name.

573 **COME UP WITH FANTASIES FEATURING LOCAL CELEBRITIES.** Take turns coming up with fantasies featuring local celebrities (for example, the local newsanchors). The fantasies can either be things you really would like to do to or with the celebrities, or funny scenarios (such as, taking the uptight female reporter and—gasp!—messing up her hair while screwing her). You will share a secret giggle each time you see that person on TV. 💜

574 **ROLL THE DICE FOR SOME DEVIOUS FUN.** Get a pair of sexy dice (they are available at most adult stores or online outlets). These naughty dice will tell you what to do, as well as where to do it to and to whom. Rolling the dice was never so much fun! 💜

575 **MAKE YOUR OWN "COUPLES" DICE.** On each side of one of the dice put an action word, such as, caress, kiss, massage, etc. On the other die, each side should contain parts of the body . . . lips, shoulders, neck, etc. Roll the dice and do to your partner whatever you roll (or your partner has to do to you whatever you roll). 💜💜

576 **TRY ANAL DICE.** This is a twist on the standard adult dice. Anal sex dice create easy and maneuverable positions and actions for the beginner anal explorer. Obviously, this game may not be right for you or your partner if either of you strongly dislike anal sex. 💜💜

CHAPTER 13

OTHER PLACES IN YOUR HOUSE

If you're like most people, you probably get most of your sexual action in the bedroom. Sure, it serves its purpose and most of the time it is really a wonderful place. But after a while it can get a bit boring. Maybe you need a change of sexual scenery, but don't want to venture too far. No worries—there are plenty of nonbedroom places in your house where you can share some intimate encounters with your partner. You will have lots of fun "christening" all these areas of the house. And you may never look at your home quite the same way again!

577 DO IT IN FRONT OF THE WINDOW, WITH THE LIGHTS OFF. This is not as daring as doing it in front of a window during daylight. Most likely, nobody will be able to see you. But just the idea that they might—or that someone could walk by and not have a clue what you are doing a few feet away—makes this exciting. ♥♥

578 GET BUSY ON YOUR BALCONY. This offers the best of both worlds: You are out in the open, in public, yet most likely your bodies are only visible from the waist up. That's the perfect scenario for giving your guy a handjob while nobody around you has any clue what you're up to. ♥♥♥

579 FOOL AROUND IN OR NEAR THE SINK. Dishes won't be the only things getting dirty! It worked in *Fatal Attraction* (well, until the whole ugly stalker obsession thing ruined it). Having easy access to water will help make things sexier (and will also aid in the postaction cleanup). ♥♥

580 ROCK ME, BABY. Ride your partner on a recliner or rocking chair. You can try out new positions that might not be possible in a bed. The recliner would probably be more comfy, but the motion of a rocking chair can help you get into a good rhythm. ♥

581 GET NICE AND COZY ON THE COUCH. Couches are great places for romance. They are comfy, soft, and roomy enough for two people (if you squeeze together, which is actually a good thing in this situation). Plus, getting physical on the couch makes you feel like teenagers. ♥♥

582 HAVE SOAPY SEX IN THE SHOWER. The shower is the perfect place for sex fun. It's warm. It's steamy. It's wet. You can even keep some scented gels and body lotions nearby. Plus, it is easy to get clean—after you are done being dirty. ♥♥♥

583 ENJOY A NEW KIND OF "TUB TOYS." Find some sex toys specifically designed for use in the water. Try out a few the next time you're sharing a bath or shower with your partner. There are even a few that are designed to look like normal bath accessories, so you won't risk embarrassment if a visitor spots them. ♥♥♥

584 GET HORNY IN THE HOT TUB. If you have a hot tub of your own, you have probably already tried this (or at least thought about it). Once you get a hot tub, it's only a matter of time before you "break it in." So, what are you waiting for? It can be especially exciting to get it on in an outdoor hot tub during the winter. The clash of hot water and cold air can create some uniquely arousing sensations. ♥♥

585 PLEASURE EACH OTHER ON THE PORCH. Share an intimate encounter on your porch. It's the perfect middle ground: You're in the great outdoors, but close enough to the safety of your house that you can make a retreat. If your porch is near the road (or there's a lot of foot traffic in your neighborhood), there's the added excitement of possibly being caught.

586 **LEARN SOME NEW STEPS ON YOUR STEPS.** For something new, try having sex on the stairs (in your own house). Generally, this is not all that enjoyable—and definitely not very comfortable, especially if you have wooden steps. But it is probably worth trying at least once.

587 **TEASE EACH OTHER ON THE TRAMPOLINE.** If you are lucky enough to have a trampoline, this is a great place to get your groove on. It provides a built-in source of motion. At night, you can also gaze at the stars afterward. (Nighttime fun also lessens the odds of being disturbed by kids or nosy neighbors.)

588 **SHARE SOME POOLSIDE PLEASURE.** Have a pool? That's another automatic choice for erotic encounters. If it is in a secluded location (or you don't mind being seen), you can have a daytime rendezvous with the hot sun keeping you warm. Otherwise, quench your desires with a nighttime skinnydipping session.

589 **DO SOME SEXY SWINGING (THE LITERAL KIND).** Hang a swing in a private and secluded place on your property and give sex on it a try. Make sure the swing is sturdy enough to hold both of you. Bring along a picnic blanket in case you decide to take things to the ground.

590 **T**RY THE ATTIC. The downsides: The attic is musty, possibly dirty, cold, and full of cobwebs. You might also need to climb over piles of junk (and dodge spiders). The upsides: Nobody will bother you, and you might just stumble over a box of old love letters from your partner or other romantic mementoes.

591 **H**EAD DOWN TO THE BASEMENT. Basements usually have good sound-muffling qualities, which can come in handy if you tend to be noisy. They may also contain some interesting surfaces (say, a workbench or gym equipment). This is definitely not the most romantic spot in the house, but the unusual surroundings might be a nice change of pace.

592 **H**AVE SOME FUN AND GAMES IN THE GAME ROOM. If you have a game room, it should be a can't-miss stop on your sexual tour. Try out a few moves at the pool table (or try out a few moves on the pool table) and come up with other fun and games.

593 **B**E REALLY BAD IN THE BATHROOM. Depending upon the size and layout of your bathroom, this may require some dexterity and flexibility. Some bathroom locales are obvious sex stops—the tub, the sink—but you may be able to come up with a few others.

594 GET KINKY IN THE GARAGE. If you and/or your partner are really into your car(s), the garage may be one of your favorite places in the house. So, why should it be left out of all the fun? You can start by having sex in (or on) your car, and then use your imagination to see what other options you can come up with. 🔥🔥

595 GO WILD IN THE GARDEN. It's grassy, it has color-ful and fragrant flowers—what more could you want? Just be alert for any honeybees. If you have a hose or watering can handy, you can wet yourselves down while watering the plants at the same time. 🔥

596 GET SOME LOVIN' IN THE LAUNDRY ROOM. Everybody knows about the washing machine (it's like a big vibrator), but the dryer can also offer advantages. The spinning motion generally is less strong, but the warm feeling can provide a cozy surface on which to have sex. 🔥

CHAPTER 14

THE GREAT OUTDOORS

Head outdoors to scout new locales for love. Not only will you be communing with nature, but you will also have an endless variety of surfaces, textures, and spaces to choose from. Throw in the variables of weather and climate, and it's like a wonderland of endless combinations. Plus, you will be surrounded by new sights, sounds, and smells—bringing a fresh feel to each encounter.

And, of course, doing it outdoors involves the risk of being caught—or at least the possibility that someone might be watching you, with or without your awareness—and that makes things more exciting. Even if you never were much of an outdoorsy type, you will probably discover that its advantages for erotic possibilities can give you a whole new appreciation for the wonders of nature. There are infinite outdoor possibilities, but you can start off trying some of these ideas.

597 GO REALLY WILD OUTDOORS. Sex educator Deborah Sundahl of Isis Media offers these tips: "Let the wilderness hear your screams. The best way to make a long drive through open stretches of barren country enjoyable is to get out of the car and make love in the wilderness! Take the first turn off the freeway; hike up to the nearest rock face (wear boots and click a stick to scatter any snakes), and let Mother Nature hear your cries of orgasmic joy." ♥♥

598 TRY SEX ON THE BEACH. This is a classic, yet it's something surprisingly few people have actually done. Many beaches are deserted at night, and fairly dark, too. The woman should wear a long, flowing skirt and leave panties at home. Go out to a nice dinner, have a little wine, and flirt with each other, knowing what's coming for dessert. After dinner, stroll down to the beach and find a deserted spot. The long flowing skirt will provide easy access for the missionary position and a surface to prevent sand from getting in all the wrong places. ♥♥

599 DO IT IN DEEP WATER. The man stands straight up, while the woman wraps her legs around his waist. Bonus for the guys: She will basically be floating, so you won't need to support all her weight. Bonus for both of you: If only your head and shoulders are above the water, nobody from the shore will be able to see exactly what you are doing (although they could probably guess). ♥♥♥

600 ENJOY A SENSUAL SUNRISE. Another option: Wake up before dawn; load blankets, pillows, and portable drinks and breakfast into the car and drive to the beach. Watch the sun rise over the water. You'll remember the moment when the sun's rays first break over the horizon for the rest of your lives. ♥♥

601 FIND OUT WHY RAIN WAS MADE FOR ROMANCE. Take a walk in the rain with your partner. Splash in the puddles, shake the shrubbery, get as wet as possible. Then go home and rub each other dry. Don't be surprised if you find yourselves getting wet again. ♥

602 GET REALLY WET AND WILD IN THE RAIN. So, you just had a good time playing with your partner in the rain. Why make yourselves wait until you get home to get romantic? Your bodies are already wet and slippery. You know what to do. ♥♥

603 BLAZE A NEW TRAIL TOGETHER. Take a hike . . . literally. A healthy jaunt together in the woods can make you and your partner thirsty for each other. If you just can't wait until you get home to have each other, find a suitable spot along the trail. (It might be wise to bring a blanket along.) ♥

604 BE A STALLION—AND RIDE ONE, TOO. When you and your partner have a free day together, visit a stable and rent two horses. Take a horseback ride along the beach or a riding trail; carry an intimate picnic, chilled drinks, and extra blankets in the saddlebags for other activities.

605 **H**AVE SEX IN A STREAM. A stream—with its gently rolling water—is the perfect place for some outdoor fun. The gentle flow of the water, the birds singing, the sun bursting through the trees—it's straight out of a romance novel, and you get to write your own sexy scene.

606 **E**NJOY A RIVER RUSH. This is a bit more risky than sex in a stream, depending upon the river conditions. Keep in mind: It might not be a wise move if either of you is not a strong swimmer or if river conditions are rough. But the faster current of the water can really up the erotic ante.

607 **K**EEP THE FIRE GOING. Light a bonfire and snuggle next to each other on a bench under a blanket together. Do a little petting of the thighs and kissing to get things going, and use that blanket for a little privacy while you roll in the firelight.

608 **T**RADE **E**SKIMO KISSES (AND MORE). Spend the day building an igloo with the kids—roll some big snowballs, and put some plywood over the top, and pack with snow (no Eskimo skills required). After they have gone to bed, sneak out there with a few candles and sleeping bags or heavy blankets—you'll be surprised how warm it will be inside, even without body heat. ♥

609 Ⓗ**AVE SEX LEANING AGAINST A FENCE.** This is one move almost anyone can do, as most people have a fence somewhere on their property (or close by). It can feel wild and naughty. Use caution: Wooden fences may have splinters, and chain link fences can have sharp edges. ♥

610 Ⓗ**AVE SEX ON OR NEAR A FOUNTAIN.** If you're lucky enough to have a fountain on your property (even a small one will do), you can enjoy some wet and wild fun. If not, you might need to scout out the nearest fountain in a public (but hopefully not crowded) location. ♥♥

611 Ⓗ**AVE SEX ON YOUR DECK.** During the day, you'll be able to enjoy sex in the warm sun—but you'll also be more likely to be spotted by neighbors. It might be better to have your decktop fun at night, in the cool air. ♥

612 Ⓗ**AVE SEX IN A HAMMOCK.** The swinging can provide a nice sensation—plus you'll be forced to lie very close together. Just be sure to test the hammock and make sure it's sturdy enough to hold your weight. ♥

613 **HAVE SEX ON A SWINGSET OR JUNGLE GYM.**
Warning: It might not be comfortable, and you will
definitely need to be flexible and strong. But it is something that not many people can say they have done. You
will never look at a playground quite the same way
again.

614 **PITCH A TENT—AND THEN HAVE FUN INSIDE
OF IT.** Don't have any wilderness areas nearby?
Go ahead and create your own romantic camping
site in your backyard. Under the vibrant light of the
brilliant constellations, be careful not to wake the
neighbors.

615 **GO SKINNYDIPPING WITH YOUR PARTNER.**
Whether you take the provocative plunge in the vast
ocean or in a small private pool, a playful naked swim
session adds a sense of risk and adventure to any
romantic getaway. Just be sure to leave your clothes in
a safe, dry spot.

616 **SHARE SOME SENSUAL FUN IN THE SNOW.** One
of you wears your longest full-length coat and take a
stroll in the snow after dark on a mild winter night.
When the mood is right, lie down in the snow, open
the coat, and use it like a blanket.

617 **GO AS WILD AS YOU WANT IN THE WOODS.**
The woods is a popular sex spot because it offers lots

of options to choose from. Roll around on the ground, go at it up against a tree—the possibilities go on and on. Just watch out for poison ivy!

618 GET FRISKY IN THE FALL FOLIAGE. Most people dread the autumn task of raking up all those pesky leaves, but you can make it more tolerable by promising yourself the two of you will make good use of that big pile of leaves once you are done.

619 TAKE A RIDE IN A TUNNEL. A lot of people dislike tunnels—whether it's because of claustrophobia or other fears, or simply because there's often no cell phone or radio reception down there. Plus, tunnels can seem endless and boring. So, make good use of that time (and the low lighting). Have yourself some underground ecstasy, and see how much fun you can have before you see the light at the end of the tunnel. Note: Don't try this if you are the one at the wheel while driving through the tunnel, unless the traffic is at a standstill.

620 GET BUSY ON A BRIDGE. Bridges offer lots of exciting elements: the peaceful sound of the rolling water, the noisy traffic whizzing nearby, and perhaps some unpredictable movements and sudden wind gusts. Just be sure to plan ahead and situate yourselves in a safe spot, away from the traffic (and any nosy onlookers).

621 GET BUSY UNDER A BRIDGE. This may or may not be safer and more pleasant, depending upon the bridge in question. You are closer to the water, but also much more likely to bump into transients who are living down there. Probably not a good idea at night.

622 EXPLORE NATURE'S SECRET HIDEAWAYS. Do like the cavemen used to, and create your own little love nest inside a cave. Be sure to find one that has not already been claimed by its more natural occupants (say, bears or other wildlife). This is one of those things that often sounds romantic, but may not live up to the hype.

623 ENJOY A REAL ROLL IN THE HAY. Here is your chance to get lucky with the farmer's daughter. If you can get some alone time in a barn, you can have fun acting out scenes from some of your favorite old westerns (or any movie involving a western-style romp in the hay).

624 MAKE LOVE ON A MOUNTAIN. Make some magic together on the top of a mountain. The view will be breathtaking (as will the thinner oxygen), so you'll get a real adrenaline rush. Plus, you will most likely be all alone and can make as much noise as you want. Get a kick out of hearing your yells and moans echo all over the mountainside.

625 **H**AVE SEX IN A WATERFALL. It doesn't need to be a huge waterfall. As long as the warm water is flowing over the two of you, it will be an exciting rush. ♥♥♥

626 **D**O IT IN THE DESERT. You don't need to trek to the Sahara. Any desert (or hot desert-like area) will do. The hot sun beating down on you will make you want to rip off your clothes—quick. ♥

CHAPTER 15

OTHER PLACES

Okay, so you (and your partner) have gotten busy everywhere in your house, and all over the surrounding property. Been there, done that. Now you are seeking new adventures and new places to do the deed.

Relax—there are lots of places you haven't "christened" yet. The entire world is out there, just waiting for you to leave your mark (so to speak). No matter what type of atmosphere or setting you might be looking for, there are plenty of options available. You just need to start looking at everything around you as a possible "passion spot." You could try a new place every day and still not run out of ideas, but here are some suggestions to get you started.

Other People's Houses

Sure, your own house is old news. Even if you have been creative and gotten cozy in every nook and cranny, at some point your own house can get boring. But other people's houses are totally new territory. Obviously, you can try hooking up at the homes of all your friends (hey, what are friends for?) as well as your family. But don't stop there. Consider the following options.

627 **HAVE SEX IN A FAMOUS HOUSE.** Having sex in a house that appears on any "Celebrity Homes" map would definitely earn you bragging rights among your social circle for quite a while. If you can manage to get busy in Brad Pitt's house (say, if your partner happens to be his gardener's cousin or whatever), that would be the jackpot. But even a "slightly D-list type of famous" house will do. Say, a house that's been featured on *Cribs*. Except for Puck's. Or that guy from *Jackass*. ♥

628 **HAVE SEX IN AN INFAMOUS HOUSE.** For example, a house that has been featured on *Cops*. Yes, this is much less glamorous than a celebrity's house, but still a good conversation starter. Hey, you gotta take your claims for fame where you can get them. ♥

629 **HAVE SEX IN THE HOME OF YOUR PARTY HOSTS.** Take your partner by surprise by sliding into the bathroom at a party as you go in. Have a short makeout session after everyone has done their business. When you come out, people will wonder what you've been up to in there. You can also sneak off into the guestroom for a quickie. Just make sure to straighten the bed before you leave.

630 ℋAVE SEX IN THE TOTALLY AWESOME HOUSE OF SOMEONE YOU DON'T KNOW AT ALL. Ask a real estate agency to find you a furnished penthouse to rent for a weekend. Hire a caterer to cook and serve all your meals. Hire a couple of masseurs to come give you twin massages. Book theater or opera tickets. Come Friday, pick your partner up from work in a limousine, and take him or her to the penthouse, where a new gown or suit awaits for the evening's festivities.

Off-Limits Places

Let's face it, there's something irresistible about going someplace you aren't supposed to be. And if you can manage to have a little adult fun while you're at it, all the better. It won't be easy to squeeze in a sex romp at any of these places—but then again, that's the whole allure of off-limits places. They tend to be a challenge. Are you up for it?

631 ℋAVE SEX ON A MILITARY BASE. Bring your man's little soldier to full attention by seducing him in a restricted area of a military base. Unless your partner is in the military, actually getting on a military base will probably be a big challenge, so you will need to get creative.

632 **HAVE SEX AT A POLICE STATION.** This is so sexy, it should be illegal (and probably is). Do you and your partner like to live dangerously? If so, this is the perfect move for you. Figure out a way to spend some time together in a police station . . . preferably without getting arrested.

633 **HAVE SEX IN THE BOSS'S OFFICE.** Sneak into work after hours, and go at it in the boss's office. Afterward, smoke one of his expensive cigars. Then be prepared to look for another job if the boss ever finds out.

Normal Dates Turned Naughty

There's nothing inherently naughty about these places—heck, your uptight Aunt Martha goes to the opera all the time while practically wearing a chastity belt. But with a little effort and imagination, you can be as bad as you wanna be.

634 **GET DIRTY AT THE OPERA.** Your man probably won't be too excited about heading to the opera—until you fill him in on you decidedly undignified plans for the evening. It won't be easy to hook up here—what with everyone being so polite and quiet—so you may need to keep the moans to a minimum.

635 **HAVE SEX AT A BOWLING ALLEY.** Head over to the nearest bowling alley for twilight couples bowling. Have fun, a couple of beers, and behave like crazy people. Make a bet. At the end of the night, the one with

the most strikes, or the least gutter balls or whatever else you decide, becomes slave to the other. ♥

636 **BE A PAIR OF WILD AND CRAZY WEDDING CRASHERS.** Get dressed to the nines, and crash a wedding or some other black-tie bash. Try to find a place where you can have a quickie. Even if you get busted, you're dressed for dinner. Be confident—act like you belong! ♥

637 **FIND OUT WHY THE ARTS CAN BE EROTIC.** Many couples enjoy appreciating the arts together. Get together for a romantic late night dinner, and then attend a midnight reading session of erotica. Go straight home afterward and work on creating your own masterpiece. ♥

638 **GET COZY AT A SPORTING EVENT.** If you absolutely hate something that your man loves, such as a certain sport, buy some tickets and accompany him to the game. He'll be bowled over that you love him enough to want to spend time with him, even if it's not your first choice of things to do together. ♥

639 **DISCOVER WHY CELEBRATORY SEX CAN BE COOL.** If your partner's favorite team wins, treat him to a private victory celebration when you get home. You can add some special touches—say, dressing up in lingerie featuring the team colors. It will make the thrill of victory all the sweeter. ♥♥

640 **ENJOY CONSOLATION SEX, TOO.** If his team loses, you can help soften the blow with some fabulous consolation sex. It will cheer him up, and almost make him forget about that painful loss. (Note: Pointing out that his team got robbed and the game was obviously rigged will also help the mood.)

Other Exciting Places

Here is an assortment of varied places where you might want to try having some fun. These places may not be totally exciting on their own, but the two of you will bring the party when you both arrive all hot and bothered and ready for action.

641 **ENJOY A SEXY SECOND HONEYMOON.** For the married folks: Surprise your spouse with plane tickets to the place you spent your honeymoon—perhaps during a different season—and plan on really exploring all of its venues. Try new restaurants, visit historical sites, and natural places—and be sure to get someone to take some pictures of the two of you having a blast!

642 **GET YOUR KICKS WHILE HAVING A FREAKY FLASHBACK.** Have your partner join you in a sleepover back at your childhood home if possible. Have sex in your old bedroom. It will be even better (in a strange way) if the room was never redecorated. Afterward, entertain your partner with embarrassing childhood memories.

643 **H**AVE A SEXY PRIVATE POOL PARTY FOR TWO.
Sneak into the swimming pool of the hotel you're staying at, long after the pool is closed for the night. Try not
to giggle (or moan) too loudly or you will risk waking
the rest of the guests.

644 **H**AVE AN EVEN BETTER (AND RISKIER) PRI-
VATE POOL PARTY FOR TWO. Sneak into the pool
of a hotel you aren't staying at. This will take a bit more
effort and ingenuity. On the plus side, if you get caught,
you do not need to worry about getting kicked out of
your room.

645 **G**O TO A PEEP SHOW. Enjoy a performance by your
own private dancer. The performers usually can't see
you, so they have no idea what the two of you might
be doing during the performance. Warning: It may be
in a bad part of town (and also may not be the most
hygienic place you've ever seen—try not to think about
who else may have been there).

646 **S**END AN OFFICIAL INVITATION FOR UNOFFI-
CIAL FUN. Use a computer to make a stylish invita-
tion, asking him to join you for dinner at a fine hotel.
You don't need an RSVP. You can say something like,
"Mrs. John Smith requests the pleasure of your com-
pany for an evening of fine dining on February 14 at the
Regency Hotel at eight o'clock." Be sure you've booked
a room upstairs!

647 **GET COZY WITH A COTTAGE GETAWAY.** Book a cottage on a lake in a place you've never visited before. Give your spouse a sealed envelope of what he should pack, and keep the location and plans a secret until you get there. Either allow your spouse to drive, giving him directions, or memorize your route so that he isn't looking at the map to the location. 🖤

648 **MAKE LOVE WHILE MAKING WAVES.** Rent a boat, assuming you know how to operate it. Take a leisurely cruise on the water. Then anchor in a private area and feel the flowing water below as you purposely "rock the boat." Don't try this if you tend to get seasick. 🖤

649 **REVISIT HIGH SCHOOL.** Find your local lover's lane, and go parking for a few hours. Make out in the car, doing as much groping and kissing as you can handle. But don't go all the way. This is about rediscovering the art of the kiss. Plus, it'll make you feel young again. 🖤🖤

650 **FIND LOVE (OR MAYBE JUST LUST) IN AN ELEVATOR.** This can involve several challenges, the first of which is getting an elevator all to yourselves (unless you want to be watched). There is also the inherent time restriction. You're pretty much limited to a quickie unless you hit the "Stop" button. 🖤🖤

651 **HAVE FUN IN A (PUBLIC) HOT TUB.** This provides all of the benefits of a hot tub (hot water, steam, the great outdoors) plus the added thrill of being in public. You may possibly even have other people in the hot tub with you, which lets you entertain your exhibition-ist tendencies.

652 GO WILD ON A WATERBED. This idea assumes that you don't own a waterbed, in which case this is old hat to you. But if you don't have a waterbed, it can be a new and exciting experience to make love on top of the rolling water. Look for a hotel with waterbeds or try to finagle an overnight invitation to the home of a waterbed-owning friend.

653 SHAKE THINGS UP ON A VIBRATING BED. This is fun to try at least once. You two will probably need to head to a hotel/motel for this one, unless of course you happen to have some kinky friends who actually own a vibrating bed.

654 GET SOME LOVIN' IN A LOCKER ROOM. The novelty of this makes it exciting, but be warned that the conditions can be pretty unsanitary. Bonus points if you can manage to get busy while there are athletes milling around. Extra bonus points if this is a locker room for a major league team.

655 HAVE SEX IN A SPORTS FIELD DUGOUT. Dug-outs aren't the most romantic of locations. For one thing, they can tend to be dusty and dirty. But you can pretend a crowd of fans is out there cheering you on from the stands. Bonus points if you head out onto the pitcher's mound and break it in. ♥

656 SCORE ON THE 50-YARD LINE OF A FOOT BALL FIELD. The risk involved here can vary greatly depending upon on the exact field in question. Hooking up on your local peewee football field probably isn't too risky (unless of course there's a game going on at the time, in which case you can get your privates stomped by a grade-schooler in cleats). On the other hand, trying to get away with this at, say, Giants Stadium would be much more of an amazing feat. ♥♥

657 GO DOWN (ON EACH OTHER) IN THE GRAND CANYON. This natural wonder is amazing enough on its own, but you will make it extra special by sharing your own private encounter in a secluded spot. Just be sure to watch out for approaching tourists (and law enforcement officials). ♥

658 HAVE A BALL AT NIAGARA FALLS. The roar of the waves, the steam from the water—the Falls are like a hot date just waiting to happen. Plus, you will be surrounded by lots of honeymooners, and all that romance is bound to be contagious. ♥♥

659 INDULGE YOUR HORNINESS BY THE HOLLY-WOOD SIGN. Talk about a claim to fame. You and your partner can star in your own private erotic show. See if you can make your own personal shooting stars.

Afterward, you can enjoy the view and try to pick out some famous homes. 🔥

660 ROCK THE RED-LIGHT DISTRICT. Head on over to the notoriously naughty red-light district of Amsterdam. In an area that is world famous for its decadence, it will be pretty tough to shock the locals. You and your partner will need to work extra hard! 🔥🔥

661 HAVE A SEXUAL SAFARI. Get busy with your partner in the jungles of Africa, while exotic animals graze all around you. What better place to "get wild" than out there in the wild? Maybe you can even teach the animals a thing or two about mating rituals. 🔥

662 HIT THE SLOPES (AND THE SHEETS) AMONG CELEBS. If you want to do the deed in the snow, there is no better place than Aspen, where you will be surrounded by lots of stars (many of whom will be there with their mistresses). Be alert for nosy paparazzi. 🔥

663 HAVE A REAL FRENCH KISS. Paris is perhaps the most romantic city in the world. Guys, this is one place your wife or girlfriend has probably always dreamed of visiting, so she will be very grateful if you take her there. Have a good time as close to the Eiffel Tower as you can get. Ooh la la! 🔥

664 GO FROM "ALOHA" TO "OH MY GOD!" in the Pacific. Get your lei—and get laid—on the beaches of

Hawaii. The Hawaiian islands are perhaps one of the most beautiful places around—and you don't even need to leave the country. Plus, it's warm pretty much all year long.

665 HAVE SEX ON SPRING BREAK. Head down to Cancun during spring break. With all the partying and hookups going on, you will fit right in. You'll feel like a teenager again—only without the fake ID. You might even win a wet T-shirt contest!

666 PICK A TOWN THAT SOUNDS SEXY. For example, the good old town of Intercourse, Pennsylvania. Or maybe someplace with a porn-sounding name like Honey Hole. Find the most romantic spot in town, and have an incredible sexual encounter. Think of the cool story you'll be able to tell.

Public Places

When looking for new places to have some adult fun, the allure of a public place is obvious: There are lots of onlookers (as in, an audience) to enjoy your performance. Even if you sneak off to a relatively private part of a public place, you still risk getting caught, which can be very exciting. The best part? You don't need to look very far to find this kind of place—there are lots of potential locations all around you. Here are a few suggestions to consider.

667 HAVE SEX IN TIMES SQUARE. If it's a crowd you want, this is the place to go. Plus, New Yorkers are pretty much unshockable. Be warned: Police patrol this area. If you want to be wimpy and take the easy route, head for one of the sex shops or peep shows. 🖤

668 **HAVE SEX IN TIMES SQUARE ON NEW YEAR'S EVE.** Think of the normal Times Square crowd multiplied by a thousand. You'll have obstacles to overcome, however: It's nearly impossible to get to unless you arrive very early, plus you'll find heavy security presence. But phrases like "watching the ball drop" or "Dick's Rockin' New Year's Eve" could take on a whole new meaning. 🖤

669 **ENJOY A VIEW TO A THRILL.** Head into your nearest big city. Enjoy the view and a kiss (or more, if you dare) at the top of the tallest building in the area. This is a traditional move straight of a classic romantic movie scene. Make your own memories. 🖤

670 **HAVE A TORRID TIME IN THE TOWER.** Know of a park near you with a lookout tower? At near dark, everyone will have climbed down, and you can have a wild time at the top in the fading light before the rangers come to kick you out. 🖤

671 **GET A HOLE IN ONE.** Get busy on a golf course, perhaps while lying in the sun on the lush greens. Be sure to have your golf cart at the ready nearby in case you need to make a quick getaway. Oh, and watch out for wayward balls. 🖤

672 HAVE SEX ON A MINI GOLF COURSE. The mini course can have an advantage over the bigger version. You won't need a golf cart, and can easily walk to your "location of love." But there's a much greater chance of being stumbled upon by an elderly couple or some youngsters.

673 RIP YOUR CLOTHES OFF AT A REST STOP. If you want raw thrills, this is about as raw as it gets. It's dirty, it might be dangerous—and you will be surrounded by horny truckers and cranky travelers. You had better make it a quickie—and bring a weapon.

674 PLAY WITH EACH OTHER ON THE PLAY-GROUND. Playgrounds can be lots of fun for people of all ages. The most challenging part is finding an empty playground. Be sure to try the jungle gym and slide—but make it quick, before any kids show up.

675 GET YOUR THRILLS BETWEEN THE BOOKS. Get busy with your partner at the local library. (Preferably not in the kids' section.) Needless to say, you will both need to keep as quiet as possible. And watch out for the librarians, who won't look kindly on your library lust.

676 CLIMB THE STAIRWAY TO HEAVEN. Try your luck on the stairway of a public building. As with the stairs at your house, comfort (or lack thereof) is a concern—as is the unsanitary environment. But the risk of getting caught adds excitement. To increase your odds of privacy, choose a building that has an elevator, as it will usually have less stairway traffic.

677 HAVE SEX IN A DRESSING ROOM. Do the nasty in a department store dressing room. To up the ante, try this at a snobby, upscale boutique. Ladies, you will never hear your partner complain about going shopping with you again! Be prepared for the possibility of being interrupted (either by an employee or another customer).

678 HIT THE DRESSING ROOM, AFTER A FASHION SHOW. Ladies, get your guy warmed up for action by modeling a few revealing outfits (ideally, ones too expensive for you to actually buy and wear at home). Make sure you are wearing sexy lingerie—or no undergarments at all—so you can flash him a few times in between wardrobe changes. When he can't stand it anymore, pull him into the dressing room for the real showstopper.

679 HAVE SEX AT A MOTORCYCLE RALLY. For example, the ones in Sturgis or Daytona. Anything goes in this environment, and you will fit right in with the rest of the wild bikers. If you don't have a bike, borrow or rent one.

680 GO CAMPING. Cuddle up in your sleeping bag and peek out of your tent to watch the stars while staying warm by the fire. It doesn't get much more romantic than this. Plus, it's a good bet there are lots of other campers around you doing the same thing. 🖤

681 𝓗AVE SEX ON THE ROOF OF A PUBLIC BUILDING. You could try the roof of your apartment building or a hotel (unless you're in the habit of checking out the roofs of random buildings). On a nice night, it'll be romantic to make love under the stars—until someone stumbles upon you and ruins the moment. 🖤

682 𝓗AVE SEX IN THE YARD OF SOMEONE YOU KNOW. It would probably be preferable (to them, at least) if they were not home at the time, but it would be tougher to access to their yard. So try figuring out a way to get busy in their yard without anybody being the wiser (perhaps sneaking off to a secluded corner during a barbecue or other get-together). 🖤

683 𝓗AVE SEX IN THE YARD OF TOTAL STRANGERS. Okay, this one might be tough to pull off. Gaining access to a stranger's yard could be a challenge (and could also possibly get you arrested). You also need to watch out for guard dogs. 🖤

684 𝓐CT LIKE A BUNCH OF STRAY CATS. Go at it hot and heavy in an alley. Hey, that's what alleys are for. But you can't be afraid to get dirty—literally. On the plus side, nobody would probably bat an eyelash if they spotted you (unless of course it was someone you know). People just expect to see all kinds of depravity in alleys, so it wouldn't be shocking to see a couple going at it.

685 **HAVE SEX IN A SUPPLY CLOSET.** The risk/challenge factor involved here can very greatly depending on the circumstances. If neither of you work in a building with a supply closet, that might be the first problem. But there is something exciting about the stereotypical supply closet sex romp that makes it alluring.

686 **DO IT AT THE OFFICE, WHILE ON DUTY.** This idea is easier to pull off if you and your partner both work in the same place—or if you at least have your own private office. It's tougher to do if your "office" actually consists of just a cubicle, or if your office has a lot of security (or nosy coworkers who tend to work long hours).

687 **HAVE SEX IN A NIGHTCLUB.** The darker (and more crowded) the nightclub, the better your chances of pulling this off without getting caught (and thrown out). If you pick a rough club in a seedy part of town, it is likely that nobody will bat an eyelash.

688 **HAVE SEX AT A FAMILY REUNION.** This idea takes a lot of courage. But it is a great way to escape from all those unbearable relatives. And if you get caught, it will be the talk of the next fifty family reunions. What will poor Grandma think?

689 HAVE SEX AT A WEDDING. There is loud music, romance is in the air—and someone else is picking up the bar tab. The tricky part is finding a quiet, isolated spot where you won't be stumbled upon by the flower girl—or the minister.

690 HAVE SEX AT A RADIO STATION. This is a bit easier to pull off if you or your partner happen to be a DJ. Otherwise, you might need to pull some strings to get access to the place. An added perk: You don't even need to bring your own music!

691 HAVE SEX AT THE AIRPORT. This is not as exciting as doing it on an airplane, and—thanks to heightened security concerns at many airports—tricky to pull off without getting busted. But on the upside, you don't need to shell out money for a plane ticket.

692 HAVE SEX IN A CEMETERY. Yes, this idea is pretty damn morbid. Sex in a cemetery might not appeal to run-of-the-mill couples, but if you're a unique pair, this might be your idea of a good time.

693 HAVE SEX IN A (SHARED) LAUNDRY ROOM OR LAUNDROMAT. Your building's laundry room or a public laundromat has all the attractions of your laundry room at home (the vibrating washer, the warm dryer) plus the possibility of having an audience. Not a good move if you don't want your neighbors knowing your business.

694 **H**AVE SEX IN A FUNERAL HOME ... preferably when no services are going on. This idea would probably appeal to the same group who would consider having sex in a cemetery. And it's best to keep it a secret, or people will probably look at you funny (and ban you from all future memorial services). 🖤

695 **H**AVE SEX IN A CAR WASH (THE DRIVE-THROUGH KIND). It's warm, there is lots of soapy water swishing around, your car is moving—and there are people waiting at the other end, so this had better be a quickie. 🖤

696 **H**AVE SEX IN A CAR WASH (THE SELF-SERVICE KIND). You are standing there washing your car, getting all soapy—it's a natural turn-on. Keep plenty of quarters on hand, and be prepared: You may also have an audience—perhaps a teenager waiting to wash his Chevy. 🖤

697 **G**ET SWEATY WITH YOUR PARTNER AT THE GYM. The gym is a good place for sex: the sauna, the pool, the showers. With all the grunting and groaning, your noises will blend right in. Just be sure to wipe everything down before and after you use it. 🖤

698 **M**AKE OUT IN THE MOVIES. Why should the teen-age crowd have all the movie magic fun? This is probably best when done in a movie intended for adults, as opposed to a cartoon that is packed with kids. 🖤🖤

699 MAKE OUT (AND MORE) AT THE DRIVE-IN.
You may see quite a few people (of all ages) around you who are doing the same thing. Start with a heavy make-out session and end up with your bare feet planted on the windows as you go at it. Other moviegoers may watch. Let them.

700 CHOOSE A SURPRISE DESTINATION. Avoid another predictable weekend by planning a trip to a city you've never visited. Determine a few destinations you both would love to visit, pick one out of a hat, and set a date. The fun of planning together, coupled with the excitement of an unexpected trip, will help to prove that honeymoons aren't just for newlyweds.

CHAPTER 16

FUN WITH FOOD

Food can play an important role in spicing up your sex life (pun intended). For one thing, food (especially good food) is a sensual experience all on its own. Combining the pleasures of food with the delights of sex is a recipe for one unforgettable experience. Whether you eat it before hitting the sheets or incorporate it into your lovemaking, food can definitely be fun. Try these tips for making edible treats part of your erotic routine.

Breakfasts and Desserts

Food doesn't need to involve an entire eight-course meal to be effective. Even small meals like breakfast and dessert can add some romance to your routine.

701 **KEEP YOUR MORNING MENU FUN.** Make yourself (and your partner) a breakfast worth waking up to. Skip the granola and juice—or, worse yet, the cold cereal. Instead, share champagne and donuts at breakfast. Maybe even add some delicious French pastries. Start your day with a bang! ♥

702 **TAKE YOUR TIME EATING (AND FEEDING YOUR PARTNER) BREAKFAST.** Make your partner breakfast in bed, and feed it to her a bite at a time, daintily dabbing the corners of her mouth. Tease her a little with the fork full of food, and kiss her in between bites. There's more than one reason it's the most important meal of the day! ♥♥

703 **ENJOY SOME CAKE AND CHAMPAGNE TOGETHER, JUST BECAUSE.** Order a special favorite cake (or one of your partner's favorite flavors) for no special occasion, but personalize it yourself with anything you want. Break out the fancy china and use cloth napkins. Serve it with champagne. ♥

704 **GET CREATIVE WITH YOUR CAKE.** There are lots of possible ways to make even a scrumptious cake

more exciting. For example, write something dirty on the cake. Save some of the icing for some tasty foreplay later.

705 SHARE AN INDECENT DESSERT. Order an adult cake (say, one in the shape of a nude woman's body or a man's genitals). Don't alert your partner to the theme beforehand. Let it be a surprise. You can fight over who gets the best piece. Enjoy your indecent treat together privately with champagne.

706 GET A CHOCOLATE FOUNTAIN. A chocolate fountain is one item that everyone should have in their kitchen (or bedroom). It's great for whipping up sensual chocolate-covered treats like strawberries, pretzels, etc. Be creative—you can cover just about anything in chocolate, so have fun and use your imagination.

707 KEEP PLENTY OF WHIPPED CREAM ON HAND. This is a staple of food-related foreplay. Best of all, it is cheap and easy to find at any grocery store. To give your partner a hint, just have the can sitting on the kitchen table when she arrives home.

708 MAKE YOUR WHIPPED CREAM A BIT WILDER. Be as creative as you can. Try tinting the whipped cream with food coloring. Or add some flavoring. Have a competition with your partner to see who can come

up with the best idea. The best part: You get to test out
all the creations.

Aphrodisiacs

We've all heard the stories about aphrodisiacs and their supposedly magical libido-boosting powers. Nobody can say for
sure whether these foods actually do affect you biologically—
but it's fun to give them a try.

709 **DO YOUR OWN APHRODISIAC TEST RUN.**
This is a fun (and tasty!) experiment to try. Make a
list of all the foods you can think of that are supposedly aphrodisiacs. Spend a week (or longer, if needed)
incorporating one of these foods into your meal every
day or night. Monitor the results and see which ones
turn up the heat for you, and which simply leave a
bad taste in your mouth. It's like having your own sexy
test kitchen! Following are some rumored aphrodisiacs
to try.

710 **OYSTERS.** Oysters are perhaps the most well known
of all stereotypical aphrodisiacs. Even if you do not particularly like eating oysters, try sampling them at least
once to see if they really live up to the hype.

711 **CHOCOLATE.** In addition to all of its other great qualities, many people believe chocolate can help put people
in the mood for romance. As an added bonus, chocolate is so versatile. You can eat it as is, drip it on other

foods—or use it to decorate each other's bodies.
💗💗💗

712 **LIQUOR.** Liquor (especially champagne and wine) is also high on the list of alleged aphrodisiacs. Not to mention, they add a romantic feeling to an event and make even a boring dinner more exciting. Plus, they also tend to help you relax and shed your inhibitions.
💗💗

713 **SPICES.** There are many spices that reportedly have libido-boosting qualities, including nutmeg and ginger. Try a few combinations and see if you can add some spice to your sex life—literally.　💗

714 **A FEW SURPRISES.** Just about anything can be an aphrodisiac in the right situation. Remember the rumors about green M&Ms? It may be hard to believe, but even arugula has been reported to have aphrodisiac qualities.　💗

715 **TRY SOME GARLIC TO GET YOUR JUICES FLOWING.** Some people claim garlic is an aphrodisiac. Plus, garlic helps to increase the body's circulation—and proper blood flow to certain areas is essential for good sex.　💗

716 **ADD YOUR OWN SPIN.** Why rely on other people's research? Make a conscious effort to watch how certain

foods affect you, as far as any increase (or decrease) in your level of sexual interest. Pay attention to the food/libido connection and see if you can identify your own unique turn-on foods. Aphrodisiacs need not be exotic or expensive: For some people, cheap junk food does the trick, and you might discover that steak puts your meat-and-potatoes man in the mood. Sometimes, it's not just the food itself that does the trick—often, it's a psychological connection, especially if a certain food triggers the memory of an exciting experience from the past.

Don't Just Eat—Put on a Show

When it comes to food and romance, it's not just what you eat, it's how you go about eating it. Even ordinary food can seem sexy if you put a little effort into how you eat or present it.

717 **MAKE IT SEXY.** Putting any type of food in your mouth can be sexy, if you do it right. No matter what you happen to be eating, make an effort to put a sexy spin on the process. Lick it very slowly, caressing the food with your lips. Really take your time and enjoy it.

718 **AMAZE HIM WITH YOUR CHERRY SKILLS.** Try to master the art of tying a cherry stem into a knot using your tongue. This will take some practice, but it is a skill that often really impresses guys (and it's a great party trick).

719 SHARE WITH YOUR PARTNER. To up the ante—and encourage your partner to get closer to you—share some food with your partner. This can involve you simply putting some food on a fork and feeding it to him (with as much sexiness as you can muster), or actually sharing food together (think the spaghetti scene from *Lady and the Tramp*).

720 USE YOUR BODY AS A SERVING TRAY. Sure, you can feed your lover in all sorts of sexy ways, but few approaches are more erotic (not to mention more direct) than using your own body as a table or serving tray. Lie down on the floor, table, or other flat (and sturdy) area, and set out a fun feast on top of yourself—making sure it's nothing too hot for comfort. You may need to enlist a trusted friend to help you "set the table" (be sure to offer to return the favor, should she ever want to try a similar thing for her partner).

721 MAKE IT SWEET OR REALLY SEXY. You can make this as mild or wild as you want by varying the clothing/nudity level and the amount or type of food. For a less risqué version, wear a bathing suit or light clothing. To increase the mouth-to-skin contact, place the food directly on your body without any plates or trays. This will force your partner to lick the food from your skin. (Warning: this idea will also greatly increase the messiness, especially if your meal involves sticky foods.)

722 ENJOYING A BUFFET WHILE BLINDFOLDED. To make things more exciting, try the "eating off some-one's body" technique while one of you is blindfolded. You will need to feel your way around your partner's anatomy for the food, which will make things much more fun.

723 GET CREATIVE WITH INCORPORATING FOOD INTO FOREPLAY. Another fun twist: Make a game out of your sexy meal by requiring your partner to come up with a creative way to incorporate each food item into erotic foreplay. Sure, it's easy with stuff like whipped cream—but requires real imagination in the case of food items like, say, spaghetti.

724 USE FOOD AS A ROAD MAP. Use whipped cream, chocolate, or other edible treats to give your partner a little guidance. Put the food on parts of your body that you want your partner to lick, touch, or otherwise pay attention to. He will appreciate the hints—and will also enjoy watching you apply the food to your hot spots.

725 MAKE AN EDIBLE EROTIC COMBINATION. Put one half of your "recipe" on your own body, and the other half on your partner's, so you can rub together to create the perfect tasty blend. For example, you can wear the chocolate syrup while he wears the cherries.

Other Tasty Treats

Here are other ways to use taste to tempt your partner.

726 DO A PRIVATE FLAVOR TASTE TEST. You're out taking care of mundane chores—getting groceries or picking up a garden hose at the hardware store. When no one's looking, slip a finger into your panties, and touch it to his tongue. Do that a few times. When you get home, get out of those panties, and push his head between your legs.

727 GO MOROCCAN. Visit a Moroccan-themed restaurant where you can freely feed each other with your hands while dining in the midst of lush fabrics. Then try to feed each other without any hands.

728 TRY SOME THAI FOOD. Besides the rich exotic flavors, Thai food also has spices that can make you hot—literally and figuratively.

729 MELT SOMETHING IN YOUR MOUTH. Literally melt each other—when playing with chocolate or other fun toys, let them melt in your mouth to create an edible body paint that can be licked off of all your intimate parts.

730 HAVE A SEXY PICNIC. Dr. Cadell's tips: Buy all your lover's favorite finger foods, hot and cold, and create a picnic in the middle of your bed. Spread out a large sheet and cover it with all the delicious delecta-bles. Take turns feeding each other, slowly licking each other's fingers sensuously. Then play "hide the honey" game. Decide who is going to be the hider and who is going to be the seeker. The hider will be the receiver of pleasure lying naked on the bed while the seeker will put on a blindfold. Then the hider must hide a dab of honey somewhere on their body and tell their lover to find it without using their hands.

731 GIVE HIM A CITRUS SHOWER. Bend an orange slice until it bursts and sprays his penis. The citrus juice will send a refreshingly cool sensation over him. This would also work with a slice of lemon or lime.

732 GIVE HER A CHERRY TICKLER. Tickle her clitoris or nipples with a cherry stem. Be careful that the ends are not too sharp. For an added twist, dip the stem in chocolate or liquor beforehand, and then lick up the trail it leaves behind.

733 DRINK HOT (BUT NOT TOO HOT!) tea while performing oral. The warm liquid—coupled with the warmth of your mouth—will give your partner an extra thrill.

734 POUR SOME HONEY ON YOUR HONEY. For a change of pace from the usual chocolate and whipped cream, some couples like to use honey as an erotic body oil. This technique tends to get sticky and messy, though, so don't be surprised if you end up stuck to your partner (along with the sheets, pillows, and everything else nearby). ♥

735 **TRY OUT THIS BONUS USE FOR BREATH STRIPS.** Some people have claimed to use breath strips (those minty dissolving kind) in or near a woman's sensitive area to give her a little rush. A breath mint or similar type of thing would probably work in a similar way. ♥

736 **ENJOY CANDY WITH FIZZ.** Candy (or soda) that fizzes in your mouth can add an exciting sensation when kissing or performing oral sex. Just stay away from Pop-Rocks, or any really small candy that can easily get lodged into small openings. Let's just say that would not be good. ♥

Using Food as an Accessory

Food can be a great sexual accessory. Here are some tips that can help you make the most of your food-related foreplay.

737 **BE CONSCIOUS OF TEMPERATURE.** Some of the following foods are typically refrigerated, so keep in mind they will be cold. In some cases, that may be part of the allure (the chill can add an exciting twist to the sensation). However, if you fear the effect will be more akin to a cold shower, you may need to plan ahead and keep the food at room temperature for a while. ♥

738 **TRY SOME EDIBLE UNDERWEAR.** You have probably always been curious about these, so why not give
them a try? They are available in different flavors, styles,
and sizes. Most people find that they aren't all that
they're cracked up to be, but they're something different to add to your same old routine. ♥

739 **MAKE A TASTY TRAIL.** Use a juicy piece of fruit
(strawberries are a good choice) to leave a line along
your partner's body. Then go back and let your tongue
follow the sweet trail. You can also do this with liquor.
♥♥

740 **JUST ADD ICE.** Ice is like a terrific all-purpose erotic
enhancer. Flick it quickly across your partner's nipples,
penis, or other erogenous zones for a breathtaking
thrill. Or hold it in place a bit longer to heighten the
effect. (Note: Be careful not to hold ice against sensitive
skin for too long, as this might become uncomfortable or even painful). Keeping some ice in your mouth
during (or immediately prior to) oral sex can give your
partner a cool tingling sensation. ♥♥

741 **TRY SOME FLAVORED NIPPLE BALM.** This does
double duty: It helps keep your nipples in good shape
while also making them pretty tasty. Ladies, your guy
will love licking this tasty flavoring off your body. ♥

742 **JUST SAY "YES" TO JELL-O.** Jell-O can make for
a great edible erotic treat. It's jiggly, chilly, and tasty.

Plus, it comes in a ton of different flavors. And it is pretty cheap and easy to make. Sounds like a sure-fire winner!

743 **USE ANATOMY TO YOUR ADVANTAGE.** The shape of the male anatomy lends itself to some creative possibilities when it comes to incorporating food into foreplay. See how many unique ideas you can come up with. Following are a few suggestions.

744 **USE DONUTS.** Donuts present some interesting possibilities. Use a donut as a penis ring and slowly nibble on it until your work your way to the surprise inside. You can also lay it on top of your woman's breasts or vagina and eat your way down to the surprise underneath.

745 **TRY USING LICORICE.** Get a long string of licorice and wrap it around him (not too tight!). For once, he will be glad you have a sweet tooth. Guys, you can also use the long strings of licorice to tickle your partner's body.

746 **DIP HIM INTO SOMETHING EDIBLE.** It's great to drip or drizzle chocolate and other edible elements on your body, but when it comes to the male anatomy, many couples find it easier and quicker to just dip the man's member into the chocolate (or, say, the jar of marshmallow filling). Obviously, you would want to then keep this "bedroom used" food hidden away in a special place, so as not to get it mixed up with your everyday kitchen supplies.

747 GET SOME ADULT MOLDS. Available in some adult toy stores, these are similar to ice cube molds, except they are in the shape of penises and boobs. You can fill them with water (to make adult-shaped ice) or add a unique touch by filling the molds with juice, flavored water—maybe even champagne.

748 CONSIDER THE FEMALE ANATOMY. Likewise, the female anatomy makes some food-as-foreplay scenarios pretty obvious. Obviously, you would want to use caution when inserting anything into the body, but when approached with care, this type of food foreplay can be both easy and enjoyable. Some examples follow.

749 PICKLES. This one needs no explanation. A pickle is basically nature's homegrown dildo.

750 CUCUMBERS. The same thing goes for cucumbers. Take some time to pick out the one that will be the perfect fit for your partner.

751 OTHER VEGETABLES. Some people trying using other vegetables—such as celery or carrots—but you may find that they don't work as well. Plus, their ends tend to be rough and/or pointed, which is not a good thing.

752 CLEAN THINGS UP IN A SEXY WAY. One downside of using food in foreplay: Many of these items
tend to get sticky or messy, especially when they start
to dry. No problem—just have your partner join you
for a sexy shower or bath.

CHAPTER 17

TAKE YOUR SEX LIFE HIGH-TECH

You gotta love modern technology. It has made virtually every area of our lives easier and more exciting. And yes, that includes our sex lives. It might be tough to imagine today, but it wasn't too long ago when lovers had to rely on old-fashioned print porn mags and love letters (sent by snail mail). Thankfully, today there are all sorts of modern ways to use technology in erotic and exciting ways. Here are some ways you can use high-tech helpers to make things sizzle in the bedroom.

753 **ENGAGE IN PHONE SEX.** This idea is so obvious, yet still so exciting. It can either be easy or very difficult, depending on how you approach it. Some people try too hard to overdo it, while others get tongue-tied and can't figure out what to say. Make it simple: Just be blunt and direct, and don't overthink it. Your partner is happy to hear you say anything, especially if you say it in an urgent, "I wish you were here with me now!" tone of voice.

754 **BE BOLD WHEN DOING PHONE SEX.** If there are things you are too shy to say to your partner face to face, take advantage of the fact that she can only hear you. Be bold, and tell her exactly what you want to do to her (or, what you are doing to yourself while thinking of her).

755 **ENGAGE IN PHONE SEX WITH SOMEONE OTHER THAN YOUR PARTNER (BUT WITH YOUR PARTNER'S PERMISSION).** Not every couple would be comfortable with this, but if you are, it can be a turn-on for your partner to see you trade X-rated talk with a stranger. Note: The stranger should be someone you never intend to actually meet (perhaps a phone sex operator or someone you found through an adult call-in line).

756 **ENGAGE IN PHONE SEX WITH A STRANGER WHILE PLEASURING (OR BEING PLEASURED BY) YOUR PARTNER.** This can be exciting for both of you, if you pull it off successfully. It is almost like being in a threesome, but without any of the hassles or complications. ♥♥♥♥

757 **SEND YOUR PARTNER RACY TEXT MESSAGES OR E-MAILS.** Tell him what you want to do to him, or want him to do to you. ♥♥

758 **CREATE YOUR OWN EROTIC ACRONYMS OR ELECTRONIC SHORTHAND.** Try to come up with your own private acronyms or online shorthand. Make a date to engage in some phone sex. ♥♥♥

759 **ADD SOME RACY PICTURES.** Generally, these would be pictures of yourself. But you could also do an online search for adult pictures, perhaps ones demonstrating a new position or sex trick you want to try with your partner. It will drive him crazy! ♥♥♥♥

760 **USE YOUR CAMERA PHONE.** Take some risqué photos and use those camera phones to entice each other while away from one another. Be as creative and daring as you like. ♥♥♥♥

761 **HAVE CYBERSEX WITH YOUR PARTNER.** If you two are in different places (and assuming neither of you is using a work computer) this can be a nice alternative to phone sex. For one thing, you don't need to be self-conscious about how you sound or if your voice is sexy enough. ♥♥♥

762 SEND EROTIC INSTANT MESSAGES. If you use IM, you can have a sexy chat in real time, and can even include dirty photos or links to adult sites.

763 HAVE CYBERSEX WITH YOUR PARTNER USING WEBCAMS. If you are both using computers with webcams, you can see (and, possibly, hear) what the other is doing. It has all the best parts of phone sex and cybersex combined, along with video capabilities thrown in for good measure.

764 HAVE CYBERSEX WITH SOMEONE ELSE (WITH YOUR PARTNER'S KNOWLEDGE). This idea is similar to the scenario of having phone sex with someone else while your partner listens.

765 HAVE CYBERSEX WITH SOMEONE ELSE, LETTING YOUR PARTNER DIRECT YOUR ACTIONS. In this scenario, your partner suggests what you say (or types things on your behalf).

766 TRY A REALLY HIGH-TECH SEX TOY. You might be surprised at how far sex toys have come. One example: the Labiator is a machine that the woman straddles. It has a vibrating dildo that moves up and down, entering in and out of the woman. Two other vibrators add to the excitement, while an attached vibrating butt plug offers something for the guys.

767 DEDICATE YOURSELF TO KNOWING ABOUT THE LATEST SEX TOY BEFORE ANYONE ELSE. Great scientific and technical minds all over the world are working long hours in a frantic quest to develop the very latest high-tech sex toy. Search the online news sites or sex toy sites for the latest advances in adult toys, and try to be among the first out there to get your hands (and other body parts) on the latest one.

768 HAVE PHONE SEX—EVEN WHEN YOU CAN HAVE THE REAL THING. Two phone lines in the home? A cell phone handy? Play this fun love game. Call your partner and surprise her with phone sex (she won't be expecting it when she is in the same house with you). Don't allow your partner to find you. This game is all about imagination and vocal sensation. Make sure that you are far enough away from each other in the home to have privacy and really let loose.

769 SKIP HELLO AND GET RIGHT TO THE PHONE SEX. Next time you are on that dreaded business trip or vacation away from each other, pick up the phone to say more than how the day has been. As soon as your partner answers the phone, skip the pleasantries and get right down to business. Start off with what you are wearing and end with what you aren't.

770 **LOOK AT ONLINE PORN TOGETHER.** You'll find plenty of choices out there, so you're sure to find some that you like no matter what your tastes. Make sure there are no kids around (and that your virus protection is up to date).

771 **LOOK AT PORN (AT THE SAME TIME, WHEN YOU ARE IN DIFFERENT PLACES).** You might need to spend a little time planning or coordinating this. You can both look at the same sites, or go your separate (online) ways and tell your partner what you see. This idea can take phone sex to a whole new level. (If you hate phone sex because you always blank out and can't think of what to say, this idea will help! Simply describe what you see in the images on your screen.)

772 **PICK OUT SOME IDEAS OF THINGS TO TRY BY CHECKING OUT ONLINE PORN.** Be sure to tell your partner about positions or techniques that look like something you might want to try with her.

773 **CREATE YOUR OWN (SEXY) AVATARS.** These are cartoon characters you create to represent yourself on websites, message boards, or online games and sites like *http://secondlife.com*. You can make them look like anything you want.

774 CREATE AVATARS THAT ARE SEXY FAN
VERSIONS OF YOURSELVES. The great thing
these fakes characters is that you can make them
any way you want. This is your chance to make y
self as sexy as you want to be.

775 GIVE YOUR AVATARS AN ACTIVE SEX LIFE.
latest thing in online games or interactive sites is
people to have sex via their avatars. The great thing
your avatars can act out things (on your behalf) tha
you do not have the nerve to do in real life.

776 GET THE GPS INVOLVED IN YOUR FOREPLAY.
Use your partner's in-car GPS system, if they have one.
Give them an address or program in a point of interest. At the other end, you can be waiting with a sexy
surprise.

777 HAVE YOURSELVES A LITTLE BIT OF RADIO
ROMANCE. Communicate only through handheld
radios for a day. Make sure to say "Over" and "Roger
that"—after you say a few X-rated things.

778 SHARE A HIGH-TECH TREASURE HUNT. Try
geocaching if you have access to a GPS. It's like a buried treasure hunt for grownups. Once you get good
at it, you can also bury your own cache—just for your
lover.

779 **PLAY WITH POWER TOOLS.** No, not those kind of power tools. I'm not talking cordless drills here. Everything has gone high-tech these days, and the world of adult toys is no exception. Today's toys don't just sit there motionless and wait for us to do all the work. You can find vibrators with variable speeds and lots of different ranges of motion. ♥♥♥

780 **CHECK OUT THE GADGETS TO HELP YOU GET OFF.** For those who are so dependent on high-tech aids that they cannot do anything the old-fashioned way (including masturbation), there are toys that emulate a gripping, stroking, and/or sucking feeling. ♥♥♥♥

781 **TRY A RACY REMOTE-CONTROLLED TOY.** We all know how guys love to hog the remote. Well, they will definitely love sex toys with remotes! Some adult toys now operate by remote control. ♥♥

782 **TRY A PAIR OF REMOTE-CONTROLLED VIBRATING PANTIES.** The woman walks around wearing her cute little panties—when suddenly she is hit by pleasurable vibrations when her man pushes the remote. ♥♥♥♥

783 **GET YOUR TUNES AND THRILLS, IN ONE.** Another high-tech toy you might want to try is a vibrator that connects with your MP3 player. It vibrates in sync with the rhythm of the music. ♥♥♥

784 **TRY BEING ONLINE EXHIBITIONISTS.** Lots of people get turned on by the idea of being watched. Find websites where couples can broadcast their sexual romps for viewers to see and enjoy. This is pretty risky, as you're putting yourself out there for the entire world to see and you never know where that footage can end up. But if the thought really excites you, try it while you're both wearing masks, hoods, or something else that obscures your face. Or position the camera (and your bodies) so that you are only visible from the neck down.

785 **BE A SWINGER (ONLINE, AT LEAST).** Join a swingers' message board. Nobody will know whether you are actually a swinger. In fact, this can be a great way to feel like you are enjoying this lifestyle, even if you aren't brave enough to actually do it. On many of them, you can read tales of exploits from actual swingers. In some cases, they will even post pictures or videos.

786 **MAKE A SURPRISE CD FOR YOUR PARTNER.** Burn a CD with some sexy songs and leave it in your partner's car as a surprise, maybe with a note attached saying, "Does this give you any ideas?"

787 **MAKE A SPECIAL MP3 COLLECTION.** Load your partner's MP3 player with their favorite songs—or, better yet, songs that have special meaning to the two of you as a couple.

788 **CREATE A "COUPLE CD."** Make a CD together. Burn songs that remind you of each other. Make two copies, and you can each keep one in your car as a constant reminder of your honey.

789 **MAKE A SEXY VIDEO FOR YOUR FAVORITE SONG.** Borrow a camera and use free editing software. It doesn't have to be professional quality—but sexiness is key. Better yet, do a little striptease!

790 **INTERRUPT HIS DAY.** Get naked, get comfortable, and call him at work. With his coworkers almost in earshot, tell him what you're doing to yourself. Come—loudly—as he sits at his desk and pretends nothing unusual is happening. This works the other way around, too.

791 **HAVE EROTIC INTEROFFICE COMMUNICATIONS.** Have cybersex by Instant Message and e-mail while you're both at work (using personal accounts). Be explicit and be nasty. Tell each other exactly what you want to do. Rush home and do it as soon as you get in the door.

792 **GIVE HIM A "COME HOME NOW!"** call. Call your partner's cell phone not long before his quitting time, and, in a suggestive voice, hint that something special is waiting at home. Don't give details or specifics. Tell him if he takes too long, you will start without him. Surprise!

793 **ENGAGE IN FOREPLAY, VIA FEDEX.** Next time your partner will be away for an extended business trip, send her a "pleasure package" via courier or overnight delivery. This package could include sexy lingerie (yours or theirs), sex toys, naughty pictures of yourself—maybe even a sexy DVD or tape you made just for her. ♥♥♥

Chapter 18

Vehicles

There is an eternal allure about having sex on or in a vehicle. Ever since cars have been around, people have been using them as portable adult playgrounds. Cars and erotica seem to have a strong connection—cars are often featured in adult magazines, porn flicks, and even in sexy music videos. There are many reasons why cars are so closely tied to sex: the hard steel, the powerful engine—or just the comfortable backseat. It can also be exciting to feel like a rebellious (and horny) teenager again. This is a category that offers endless possibilities—name any kind of motor vehicle, and someone somewhere has had sex in or on it at some point. Take a few of these ideas for a spin.

794 **H**AVE SEX IN A PARKED CAR. You will feel like a teenager again—especially if you fumble around cluelessly, and do this after guzzling a few cheap beers or wine coolers. For the full effect, have some heavy metal music playing loudly on the radio.

795 **H**AVE SEX IN A PARKED CAR IN A SEMI-PUBLIC LOCATION. For example, a rest stop or the edge of a public park. The possibility of getting caught adds to the excitement. Just be sure to keep the doors locked and the keys in the ignition, should you need to make a quick getaway (say, if the cops show up, or some teenagers spot you and attempt to capture some footage on their cell phones).

796 **H**AVE SEX IN A PARKED CAR IN A REALLY PUBLIC LOCATION. Say, the parking lot at Disney World or that prime spot directly in front of Macy's. Getting caught is more than a possibility—it's a definite. Now you've officially crossed the line from slightly daring to totally reckless. Still, you will have a unique story to tell when you get back from vacation (or from jail). The risk rating depends on whether or not the police get involved.

797 **H**AVE SEX IN A TOUR BUS, WITHOUT YOUR PARTNER. Okay, you shouldn't try this idea unless you're single. Or unless you and your partner have already hammered out one of those "free pass" deals.

You know, where you each grant the other permission to have sex with a specific unattainable celebrity object of your desire. Well, this is what your husband gets for underestimating your ability to talk your way onto Bon Jovi's bus. 🖤🖤🖤

798 **HAVE SEX WITH YOUR PARTNER IN A TOUR BUS.** This idea is much less risky—and requires much less work on your part (no need to flash your boobs at the security dude). The challenge will be getting access to a tour bus without servicing a band member. Just remember to apply antibacterial sanitizer liberally to all surfaces before touching anything. 🖤🖤🖤

799 **HAVE SEX IN A MOVING VEHICLE.** If you or your partner is driving, this can be risky—both for the two of you and for the unfortunate pedestrian who happens to be anywhere near your car. But assuming he can still manage to operate the car safely, going down on your man in the car (ideally, while traffic isn't moving) can be a real rush. 🖤🖤🖤🖤

800 **HAVE SEX ON TOP OF A (NONMOVING) VEHICLE.** Do it on the roof or hood of a car, and you'll feel like you're in a Whitesnake video—or possibly a bad porno, especially if the vehicle in question is a muscle car with a bad paint job. Just be warned: You may need to come up with a plausible explanation for that ass-shaped dent in the hood. 🖤🖤🖤🖤

801 **H**AVE SEX ON A MOTORCYCLE. One that's not moving. Hell, even Evel Knievel never tried that. Warning: A motorcycle is not the most comfortable surface on which to have sex.

802 **H**AVE SEX IN A POLICE CAR. If you and your partner find yourselves in the back of a police car, you're probably already in trouble, so what's one more offense to add to your rap sheet? And if you happen to spot an unattended police cruiser and get the urge to jump in the back seat—remember, those seats generally can't be opened from the inside, so you may be trapped in an embarrassing situation when the cop returns.

803 **H**AVE SEX IN THE BACK OF A LIMO. If you didn't already check this off your list after the prom, now's your chance to rectify that situation. Having sex in the back of a limo will make you feel like a VIP.

804 **H**AVE SEX IN THE BACK OF A LIMO—BEFORE YOU ARRIVE AT A BIG EVENT. Remember the gasps when Angelina arrived at an awards show and announced that she and Billy Bob had just had sex in the limo? You can experience the same thrill—and take the same risk of arriving to your big event looking like you were just ridden hard.

805 **H**AVE SEX IN A TAXI. This idea is kind of in the same vein as a limo, but on a much cheaper (and possibly much less sanitary) scale.

806 HAVE SEX ON A YACHT. This idea offers all the allure of any water vehicle, plus the ritz factor of being surrounded by luxury. ♥♥

807 HAVE SEX ON A SMALL BOAT. A rowboat, canoe, or other small boat can be an interesting place to have sex. It's usually tight quarters, and the rocking can add a nice rhythm. However, small boats can be unstable, which can make sudden or violent movements a bit precarious. On the upside, you will feel like you're in an old romantic movie. ♥♥

808 GET IT ON IN A GONDOLA. If you happen to be in Venice, this is a no-brainer. Otherwise, it might take a bit of effort. Most likely, you will only be able to find a gondola in a larger city on or near the water. ♥♥

809 HAVE SEX ON A JET SKI. If you can pull it off, you will probably be the only one in your circle with this claim to fornication fame. The risk factor depends on whether or not you sustain life-threatening injuries. ♥♥♥

810 HAVE SEX IN AN EXPENSIVE SPORTS CAR. Frankly, this is overrated. Most sports cars are too tiny to allow for comfortable maneuvering. Plus, if it's a really expensive car, the owner is probably pretty uptight about making sure it doesn't get messy. Still, it's cool to try this at least once, so you can always rent a sports car and give your partner a very special ride. ♥♥♥

811 **HAVE SEX IN THE BACK OF A PICKUP TRUCK.**
Assuming that the tailgate is sturdy enough, one of you can lie in the back of the truck with your legs hanging down over the tailgate while your partner services you.

812 **HAVE SEX IN AN AMBULANCE.** Presumably, you would not try this while you are being whisked to the hospital for a medical emergency. But if you can get access to an ambulance when it is not in use, it provides several sex-friendly assets: a bed, a pillow, some rubber gloves, even a siren. Just try not to think about the possibility of any body fluids that may have been left by previous occupants.

813 **HAVE SEX ON AN AIRPLANE.** Yes, it's cliché and predictable. But if you have an opportunity to join the Mile-High Club and do not jump on it, you will always regret it.

814 **HAVE SEX IN THE FIRST-CLASS SECTION OF AN AIRPLANE.** The accommodations are much nicer up there. Bonus points if you can manage to do this if you don't have a first-class ticket.

815 **HAVE SEX IN THE BACK OF A VAN.** Admit it, you have always wanted an opportunity to use the phrase, "If this van's a-rocking, don't come a-knocking." Vans were made for sex, so don't let all that room go to waste.

816 ROCK YOUR WORLD IN AN RV. This is like a van, only you can cook your partner breakfast (or ditch him to watch TV) immediately afterward. 🖤🖤

817 HAVE SEX IN A DELIVERY TRUCK. The sexiness of this totally depends on the type of delivery truck and the cargo it hauls. Toilet paper: not so exciting. Furniture: better, since you have a comfy surface. Beer truck: the jackpot—you've got a bar on wheels. 🖤

818 HAVE SEX IN YOUR PARENTS' CAR. If your folks have had this car for a while, it just might have been one you used for sex romps as a teen. Keep in mind, though—your parents may have also tried out the back seat a few times. 🖤

819 HAVE SEX IN A TRACTOR TRAILER. Sex in a semi can be hot, especially if it has a sleeping area, in which case it's like a truck and hotel in one. See how many truck stops you can christen during a road trip. Feel free to hit the air horn after each score. 🖤🖤🖤

820 HAVE SEX ON A ROLLER COASTER. This will probably involve violating a few safety rules, and could pose the risk of bodily harm. But having sex on a roller coaster is like getting two thrills in one. 🖤🖤🖤

821 HAVE SEX INSIDE A RACECAR. If you or your partner is a racecar driver, this idea is a bit easier to pull off—but still pretty sexy nonetheless. Be warned:

Racecars may look all hot and sexy from the outside, but inside they are cramped, hot, and not very comfy.

822 **HAVE SEX INSIDE OF A HUMMER.** What is the appeal of sex in (or on) this vehicle? Well, let's see—it's big, it's bad—and, hell, it's called a Hummer.

823 **HAVE SEX IN A SCHOOL BUS (PARKED, AND WITH NO KIDS IN SIGHT).** Yes, it's roomy, but you'll probably feel like a perv—and you may just roll over onto a wad of gum.

824 **HAVE SEX IN A LUXURY SUV.** This offers all the room of a plain old SUV, with the luxurious touches of a fancy sedan. Enjoy the feel of those leather seats (or, better yet, heated seats) against your naked skin. This is like a luxury hotel suite on wheels.

825 **HAVE SEX IN A CORVETTE.** This is a thrill, especially for the car freaks out there. Corvettes are the ultimate "hot car." Sure, they're teeny tiny. But they're sexy as hell.

826 **HAVE SEX ON A BICYCLE, IF YOU CAN FIGURE OUT HOW.** Frankly, this isn't all that sexy—and is pretty damn uncomfortable (unless you have one of those banana seats). Watch out for those pesky handlebars that will tend to poke you in all the worst places.

827 ℋAVE SEX ON A (NONMOVING) ATV. You just gotta love the versatility and usefulness of an ATV. They are great for getting to all those out-of-the-way spots in the woods. Plus, the ride has a lot of bumps and vibrations. ♥

828 ℋAVE SEX IN A (REALLY) OLD CAR. There is something really intriguing about getting down and dirty in a car straight out of *The Waltons*. It may not be sexy or flashy, but most likely it will be way more roomy than today's models. ♥

829 ℋAVE SEX ON A SUBMARINE. This would probably be tough, unless you're in the Navy (in which case you probably have other important things to do). ♥

830 ℋAVE SEX ON A CRUISE SHIP. The sexiness depends on the ship and the other people on it. Honeymooners are good; a bingo convention full of senior citizens is not quite so hot. ♥

831 ℋAVE SEX ON A MOTORBOAT. The vibrations of the roaring engine will get your motor running too! ♥♥

832 ℋAVE SEX IN A HELICOPTER. Ah, the allure of a chopper. It has all the benefits of a plane, with a little bit of added scariness. Oh, and the fact that you'll probably be about three feet away from the pilot is sure to make things interesting. ♥♥

833 **HAVE SEX IN A FAMOUS CAR.** The fact that the vehicle is well known is the thrill here, not anything about the car itself. Any famous car will do: the *Knight Rider* car, the *A-Team* van, even the Cunninghams' car from *Happy Days*. ♥

834 **HAVE SEX ON A RIDING LAWN MOWER.** Good news: hard steel surface (possibly with a slightly comfy seat), strong vibrations. Oh, and you can get your lawn work done while you're at it. Bad news: sharp, rapidly moving parts. Attempt this at your own risk. ♥♥♥

835 **HAVE SEX IN A HEARSE.** Admittedly, most people would find this creepy, if not repulsive. But if you have a morbid sense of humor, or have goth tendencies, it might be your idea of a honeymoon suite. If you can get your hands on a hearse (unoccupied, of course), this might be the perfect place to let your dark side go wild. ♥

836 **HAVE SEX ON A RIVERBOAT CRUISE.** You will feel like the true Delta queen. On the upside, these tend to move slowly, so big waves and severe rocking motions are usually not a problem. ♥

Sexy Vehicle Accessories
Cars and other vehicles tend to be sexy all on their own. But you can add another element of sexiness by using some special accessories.

837 **HAVE SEX ON TOP OF A BEADED SEAT COVER.** These knobby things were all the rage. Granted, they are not very comfy. But they will definitely provide a unique experience.

838 **HAVE SEX ON A FURRY SEAT COVER.** Now, this is more like it. These things were made for shagging. Not to mention, they keep exposed skin from getting too chilly.

839 **GET INTIMATE ON OR NEAR A FURRY/FUZZY STEERING WHEEL COVER.** This soft, comfy covering makes the steering wheel a bit less painful when it digs into your back. But you still need to be careful to avoid leaning on the horn—unless you want to alert the neighbors to your activities.

840 **HAVE SEX ON SOFT LEATHER SEATS.** This scenario actually might be a little sexier in your fantasies, as leather tends to get hot in warm temperatures—which isn't necessarily a good thing when naked skin is involved.

841 **HAVE SEX ON WARM HEATED SEATS.** Now, these are perfect for autoerotic encounters. They keep the chill away and make auto encounters a possibility even in the middle of winter.

842 **HAVE SEX IN A CAR WITH REALLY LOUD THROBBING SPEAKERS.** Crank up the music loud enough for the whole car to shake. You will feel like you are taking a ride on one big vibrator on wheels. 🖤

843 **HAVE SEX IN A CAR WITH BAD SHOCK ABSORBERS.** Sure, worn-out auto parts aren't normally sexy, but in this case, those crappy parts will add lots of extra bounce to the car. 🖤

844 **FOOL AROUND IN FRONT OF THE FUZZY DICE.** If you actually have these in your car, try to save face by using them as a sexy toy. They're big and fuzzy—surely you can think of something. 🖤

845 **CREATE THE RIGHT MOOD WITH CAR AIR FRESHENERS.** Believe it or not, some people find the smell of car air fresheners to be hot. Plus, it's a cheap way to add some cool fragrances to the setting. 🖤

CHAPTER 19

CLOTHING AND PROPS

Clothing and props can really give your sex life a big boost. Clothing—especially the right clothing—can sometimes be sexier than wearing nothing at all. And props can be both decorative and functional. Together, they make for a really exciting encounter. The best part? Chances are, you already have many of these things—or can easily get them. Many of these ideas can be used to help carry out the scenarios described in the previous sections on fantasies and role-playing.

846 SLEEP IN THE NUDE—AS OFTEN AS YOU CAN. Not only does it increase between-the-sheets sexiness (and make a middle-of-the-night or early-morning interlude easier and more likely), it also helps you become more comfortable with your own body. Plus, it gives you an excuse to snuggle—a great way to ward off nighttime chills.

847 TAKE TURNS SLEEPING IN THE NUDE. One of you sleeps naked, and the other one gets to enjoy the benefits. The nude partner must employ as many techniques as possible to try and get the partner undressed.

848 BREAK OUT THE LINGERIE. Let's start simple. You probably have some lingerie in your house—even if it's buried in your bottom drawer. Wait are you waiting for? Put those lacy little things to good use.

849 FIND OUT WHY NONLINGERIE UNDIES CAN BE SEXY, TOO. You know, those tiny little bikini briefs and white tanktops? Your guy probably finds those things sexy, too. With the right attitude, anything can be sexy—so go ahead and prance around in your "plain" underwear.

850 TREAT HER TO SOME SEXY CLOTHING. Men, give your partner a gift card for a lingerie store and send her shopping. Be sure to tell you expect her to put on a fashion show for you, so you can see her model her selections.

851 MAKE HER INTO AN UNDERCOVER LOVER. Buy her some long boots with stiletto heels, fishnet stockings, and a garter. Have her wear these under a long, conservative skirt when you go out to dinner with friends, so that only the two of you know what she's got on under her skirt. Things will get interesting when you get home.

852 DON'T FORGET SOMETHING SEXY FOR HIM TO WEAR. Ladies love lingerie, but they often forget that their guy needs something sexy for the bedroom, too. Pick out something sexy for your man to wear. This can be anything that you (or he) finds sexy, so pick whatever suits your tastes.

853 WEAR HIS UNDERWEAR. Here's a tip from Dr. Cadell: "The next time you've got a load of clean laundry to take out of the dryer, sneak off with a pair of your lover's sexiest underwear. For whatever reason it just feels kind of wild and fun to wear unusual underwear. Be daring and wear your lover's underwear to work or out to dinner. The idea is to wear it where it's least expected—and to let him find out while he is seducing you, removing your clothes piece by piece. His expression and reaction will be priceless."

854 GIVE YOUR GUY SOME JUNGLE PRINTS. If you (or your partner) have the nerve, try some jungle print thongs or tiny bikinis. Then you can feel free to act on your animal instincts.

855 SEE IF YOU CAN MAKE SILK BOXERS SEXY, TOO. Not daring enough for jungle bikinis? Silk boxers can be hot, too, especially if they are just snug enough to show off the goods. 🖤🖤

856 DRESS UP OCCASIONALLY, GUYS. Especially for blue-collar guys, dressing up may be something saved for weddings and funerals. Break that habit and get dressed up just for the heck of it. She'll want to take you out to dinner to show you off (and then come home and rip those nice clothes right off you). 🖤

857 SHOW YOUR SUPPORT IN A SPECIAL, SEXY WAY. Wrap yourself up naked in the flag of his (or her) favorite football team and help them celebrate a win—or get over a loss. 🖤🖤

858 BORROW HIS SHIRT. Greet him at the door in nothing but one of his white dress shirts, unbuttoned most of the way, when he comes home from work. Plan on having a late supper. 🖤🖤

859 BE AN S&M MODEL. Stun and amaze him by waiting in your bedroom in full S&M regalia, complete with makeup and hairstyle to match, and a few of the "tools." You don't have to use them, just look like you might. See where it takes you! 🖤

860 WEAR HIS NAME ON YOUR ... ass. Buy a pair of personalized underwear. When he sees his name

across your sexy panties, he'll be unable to tame his wild desires. 🖤🖤

Everyday Items Used as Props

With enough imagination, you can turn just about anything into a sex prop. Here are a few ideas on how to use household items as exciting bedroom accessories.

861 **DISCOVER WHY DUSTERS CAN BE FUN.** You probably hate dusting, but you will see your dusters in a whole new light once you realize they make great "ticklers" as part of your foreplay routine. 🖤

862 **BUST OUT THE BELTS.** A belt is a natural accessory for spanking and S&M. Just be sure not to be too rough. 🖤

863 **TIE ONE ON.** Wear one of his neckties—and nothing else. It will make him hot, and he just may start a special collection of "lucky ties." 🖤🖤

864 **TIE ONE ON, PART TWO.** You can also use neckties as a blindfold, or as a restraint for bondage fun. 🖤🖤

865 **USE JEWELRY AS A SEX TOY.** Take one of your necklaces or bracelets (preferably one with smooth beads or pearls—nothing sharp or scratchy) and wrap it around your man's package. Use your hand to roll it up and down his shaft. The friction will make for an incredible sensation. 🖤🖤

866 ADD SOME VISUAL STIMULATION TO THE JEWELRY MOVE. For added visual stimulation, do #865 directly after removing the jewelry from around your neck. Knowing that it had just been nestled in your cleavage will be an added turn-on for him. Plus, your body heat will add a warm feeling.

867 WARM IT UP BEFORE USING JEWELRY IN FOREPLAY. If you're planning a morning encounter, keep the necklace under your pillow. It will be nice and toasty when the time is right.

868 USE A SCARF. A silky scarf can enhance your sex life in a bunch of different ways. First, just simply running it lightly over your partner's body can feel great (unless, of course, your partner is extremely ticklish).

869 USE A SCARF FOR A RESTRAINT. You can also use the scarf to tie your partner's hands together, thus leaving him at your mercy.

870 USE A SCARF ON HIS SHAFT. Tie the scarf around your man's member (gently!). If you do this before he is fully erect, it can be an exciting sensation for the scarf to become tighter as he becomes aroused.

871 USE LOTS OF SCARVES. If you're into S&M/bondage, use several scarves to tie your partner to the bed or elsewhere. (Remember, though, only to tie them as tightly as is comfortable for both of you.)

872 **HOLD YOUR PARTNER CAPTIVE.** Tie your partner to a chair and make him request what he would like you to do to him while he is being "held captive." A blindfold could make this activity more intriguing.

873 **TIE YOURSELVES TOGETHER.** You can also use a scarf (or several) to tie yourselves together. Try it while naked, either facing each other or with one behind the other. Try to go about normal activities and make it a game to see how long you can go without progressing to any kind of sexual encounter.

874 **USE A SCARF TO DO DOUBLE DUTY.** A scarf can also be used as a great blindfold. But no peeking!

875 **USE BLINDFOLDS.** Speaking of blindfolds, they're very popular lovemaking accessories. Many people find it's easier to loosen up and relax when their partner can't see what they're doing.

876 **A SLEEPING MASK MAKES A GREAT SUBSTITUTE.** If you don't happen to have a blindfold, a sleeping mask can make a great substitute.

877 **TAKE TURNS WEARING THE BLINDFOLD.** On the other side of the coin, it can be very arousing to just lie back and anticipate the feelings of what's to come, when you have no clue what your partner is about to do.

878 **TRY SOME BEDROOM FUN WHEN YOU'RE BOTH BLINDFOLDED.** To really heighten the mystery (and increase the challenge), try fooling around when you are both blindfolded.

879 **TRY USING EARPLUGS.** Having sex while you can't hear anything will be both exciting and frustrating (in a good way). It will also heighten your other senses.

880 **USE BLINDFOLDS AND EARPLUGS AT THE SAME TIME.** If you can't see or hear, you'll be forced to feel your way around (and will also enjoy tastes and smells that much more).

Costumes and Uniforms

Perhaps the most obvious way to use clothing as part of sex play is to don costumes or uniforms to help with role-playing. Here are some costumes that should be fairly easy to find.

881 **CHEERLEADER.** If you weren't a cheerleader, you can usually find these uniforms at a Halloween store or costume shop.

882 **NURSE.** Try a secondhand store. You can also buy scrubs just about anywhere.

883 **ROCK STAR.** Have you seen the way rock stars dress these days? Take the grungiest thing from the bottom of your closet, add some ripped jeans and maybe some costume jewelry and you're good to go.

884 DOCTOR. Look for scrubs, or try to find a white coat at a medical supply store or uniform shop. ♥

885 ATHLETE. Sporting good stores are good places to find jerseys and other athletic attire. ♥

886 DOMINATRIX. This outfit is a little tougher. You will probably need to visit an adult store or an S&M website to find what you need.

887 HOOKER/STRIPPER. This one's easy. Just look for the trashiest store around, or head to the largest lingerie shop in the area. ♥

888 SCHOOLGIRL. Scour thrift stores for school uniforms, or just wear a really short skirt and knee-high socks. ♥

New Spins on Clothing

When it comes to sex, sometimes it's not what you wear but how you wear (or maybe how you don't wear it).

889 HAVE AN "EVERYTHING BUT..." fashion show series. Hit the sheets naked, except for one thing. Vary the item: one night it's shoes, the next it's a cowboy hat or a full-length coat. Find creative ways to have sex while working with (or around) that item.

890 STICK WITH WHAT WORKS WHEN IT COMES TO CLOTHING/COSTUMES. If you or your partner has a favorite piece of your partner's clothing (say, if he loves seeing you in your red high heels), trying wearing that item every night for a week during your sex romps, finding creative ways to vary your look each night. 🖤

891 **FOCUS ON VARIETY.** Wear only one thing to bed every night, but to heighten the sensual experiences, be sure to vary the textures and materials. Fur is a good choice (faux fur is fine). Leather, silk, and satin can also work well. 🖤

892 **GO COMMANDO—AND KEEP IT A SECRET.** Even if nobody else knows your naughty secret, you will still feel daring. 🖤

893 **GO COMMANDO—AND TELL YOUR PARTNER.** It will drive him crazy all evening. 🖤🖤

894 **GO COMMANDO—AND HELP YOUR PARTNER MAKE THAT DISCOVERY.** Without telling your partner outright, let him know you're uncovered down there. Perhaps by giving him a quick flash, or letting him brush up against you closely enough to get the message. 🖤🖤🖤

895 **TRY SOME BONDAGE TAPE.** This sticky material is used as restraints for sex play, but can easily be ripped apart if necessary. 🖤🖤

896 **USE WRIST AND ANKLE RESTRAINTS.** These restraints are great for everything from light bondage fantasies to hardcore S&M stuff.

897 **PUT ON A PENIS PUPPET SHOW.** Guys, this is sure to keep your partner entertained. You can make your own puppets or buy them at an adult toy store.

898 **HAVE FUN WITH FEATHERS.** Feathers can be used in all sorts of ways. Best of all, they're usually easy to find.

899 **TRY SOME TICKLERS.** The "real" ones can be found at sex stores, but you can easily improvise with stuff around your house.

Chapter 20

Sights and Sounds

Your body reacts to stimulus from all five senses. But when it comes to getting excited the quickest, it's probably related to the things you see and hear. There are lots of ways that your eyes and ears can help get some of your other body parts fired up.

Talk Dirty to Me

What's one of the sexiest sounds your partner can hear? Your own voice. It doesn't even need to be a sexy voice (although that certainly wouldn't hurt). Just hearing you say something—anything—is a vast improvement over dead silence. So feel free to make noise, lots of noise. Here are some suggestions to help you get started.

900 **SAY SOMETHING—ANYTHING.** If you read any sex-related survey, you will surely see "too-quiet partner" as one of the top turnoffs. Nobody likes performing to a silent audience. Make your pleasure known, loud and clear.

901 **SAY SOMETHING DIRTY.** Turn the dirty talk up a notch. Add a few more four-letter words. If you are usually more timid, hearing you utter naughty words like "pussy" or "cock" will be a huge turn-on.

902 **USE A FORCEFUL TONE.** Don't be so nice. Be a little rougher—give orders, add an urgent tone.

903 **TRY SOME BABY TALK, LADIES.** Some guys are turned on by this, others aren't. Give it a shot and see which camp your man is in.

904 **HOLLER OUT "WHO'S YOUR DADDY?"** This one is for the guys—and, again, your partner may love it or hate it.

905 **LEARN SOME NEW WORDS.** Expand your vocabulary. Watch a few porn movies or read some adult magazines to brush up on your sexy slang. Bust out with a few dirty words your partner has never heard you use before.

906 **GIVE DIRECTIONS.** People (especially men) often complain that they do not how to please their partner because they're clueless as to what their partner wants. Don't leave it up to guesswork. Tell your partner exactly what you want. No long-winded explanation is needed. A simple, "Put your tongue there—now!" should do the trick.

907 **SOUND EFFECTS WORK WELL, TOO.** Words aren't always needed. Feel free to add some moans, yells, gasps, or other sound effects that make it obvious just how much you're enjoying yourself.

908 **ASK QUESTIONS—BUT NOT TOO MANY.** It's great to ask, "Does this feel good?" or "Harder?" But peppering your partner with too many questions at an inappropriate time can be distracting and annoying.

909 **USE A SEXY ACCENT.** Try a few different ones until you find one that really drives your partner wild.

910 **LEARN AN X-RATED PHRASE IN A FOREIGN LANGUAGE.** Even if your partner doesn't know exactly what it is you're saying, she will probably still get turned on. ♥

911 SAY YOUR PARTNER'S NAME. This adds a great personal touch—especially as part of a sensual utterance like, "Oh, Rick, that feels so good!" Your partner will know you are totally focused on him. ♥♥♥

912 SAY SOMEONE ELSE'S NAME—AT YOUR OWN PERIL. We all know that saying—or worse, shouting—someone else's name during an intimate moment with your partner is a dealbreaker. Mentioning anyone else's name—especially a previous lover—in any context in the bedroom is very risky. ♥♥♥♥♥

Sexy Sights

Seeing something you find attractive or sexy is probably the easiest and quickest way to get turned on. This is especially true for men, who tend to react quickly to visual stimulus. We have already covered the obvious visual stimulus (porn), but here are more sexy sights that might get you in the mood.

913 GIVE YOUR PARTNER JUST A GLIMPSE OF SKIN. Sometimes seeing a fleeting glimpse of skin is just as exciting as nudity. If your partner catches a glimpse of breast, ass, or other body parts, it can easily trigger a reaction. ♥♥

914 WATCH YOUR PARTNER'S DAILY GROOMING ROUTINE. Many people find it sexy to watch their partner shaving, doing their hair, or otherwise engaging in a grooming routine. ♥

915 WATCH THE START OF SOMETHING SEXUAL. We've discussed the turnons involving watching someone have sex (whether in person or via porn). But sometimes just seeing the early moves—a couple passionately kissing, or sneaking off to a private corner—can get your imagination fired up, and you find yourself wanting to do what they will soon be doing. ♥♥

916 SEE (OR SHOW) SOME CLEAVAGE. It doesn't really matter whose it is, or how they happen to see it. For guys, cleavage is like a libido jumpstart. To get your guy going, just "accidentally" flash some cleavage. ♥♥♥

Add the Right Tunes

A great soundtrack can go a long way toward establishing the perfect mood. Putting some thought into your sensual sounds can pay off in a big way.

917 RECORD YOUR OWN SONG. If you have the talent and equipment, this is a surefire way to score. ♥♥♥

918 HAVE SOMEONE ELSE RECORD A SONG JUST FOR YOUR PARTNER. If you can't do it yourself, this option is the next best thing. ♥

919 GET THAT SONG PLAYED ON THE RADIO. She'll brag about it to her friends and you'll be a hero. ♥♥

920 GET THAT SONG PLAYED ON THE RADIO, IF IT HAS HER NAME IN IT. You will have a free bedroom pass for eternity.

921 GO WITH SENSUAL CLASSICS. Try a CD designed exclusively for romance. There are the classics, like anything by Barry White. But some people prefer instrumental tracks, so as not to be distracted by lyrics.

922 MAKE YOUR SOUNDS A BIT SEXIER. Try a CD designed deliberately for hot sex.

923 TRY A TANTRIC CD. The soothing sensual sounds are designed for sacred lovemaking.

924 BE CREATIVE WITH THE TUNES. Think of it as the soundtrack to your sex life. Don't be afraid to be unique. If you are reliving that great sex you had on the beach (or just want to pretend you are having sex on a tropical beach somewhere) then you might want to try a "sounds of the ocean" CD.

925 CHOOSE SONGS WITH MEANING. Impress your partner by picking songs that have special meaning for the two of you. Perhaps the first song you made love to, or your wedding song.

926 DANCE TO THE MUSIC. Here's a secret all exotic dancers know: The right music can go a long way in getting you in the mood to putting on a sexy show.

Choose your sexy playlist and strut your stuff in a sexy dance routine or striptease for your partner. More specific suggestions follow.

927 **"STRUT," BY SHEENA EASTON.** The name says it all.

928 **"YOU SHOOK ME ALL NIGHT LONG," BY AC/DC.** It's impossible not to strut your stuff with this song blaring.

929 **"POUR SOME SUGAR ON ME," BY DEF LEPPARD.** Every stripper has this song in her rotation.

930 **"TALK DIRTY TO ME," BY POISON.** Because it's just so damn appropriate.

931 **"WILD THING," BY TONE-LŌC.** There is no question what this song is about, and it's almost impossible to sit still when you hear it.

932 **"I TOUCH MYSELF," BY THE DIVINYLS.** Play this while talking to your partner on the phone. Ask, "Can you guess what I'm doing?"

Movies Can Help Set the Mood

Like music, movies can also help you get in the mood for sex. Porn is the most obvious strategy, but less graphic mainstream films can also work well.

Sexy Movies

Sexy films—or films with some standout sex scenes in them—can really help your partner get the hint.

933 **DEVISE YOUR OWN RATING SYSTEM.** Just like you did with the porn movies, rate movies for their level of sexiness. This time you might need to be more creative with the factors to consider. Say, one point for each "almost" glimpse of a breast, two points for each actual breast sighting, etc.

934 **HOST YOUR OWN HOT MOVIE FESTIVAL.** Pick your seven favorite erotic movies, and act out the steamy scene from one film each night for a week. You will feel like a sexy star! Here are some ideas to get you started.

935 **WILD THINGS.** Whether you want a threesome or just want to pretend you do.

936 **9½ WEEKS.** You will never look at food the same way again.

937 **RISKY BUSINESS.** Subways were never so sexy.

938 **SHOWGIRLS.** No explanation necessary!

939 **UNFAITHFUL.** It may be a film about cheating, but this movie has some of the hottest passion scenes in recent memory.

940 *BODY HEAT.* Still one of the hottest films around.

Funny Movies

Funny flicks can be effective in their own way. By helping you share a few laughs with your partner, these films can pave the way for a more intimate evening.

941 *AMERICAN PIE.* You will laugh, mostly out of relief that these things have never happened to you.

942 *WHEN HARRY MET SALLY.* This one's got the most well-known orgasm scene in all of cinema.

943 *THE 40-YEAR-OLD VIRGIN.* Even the solo sex scenes will crack you up.

Chapter 21

For the Daring

Some people really like to live on the edge and take everything one step farther than the average Joe. If you are one of those "balls to the wall" types of people, no ordinary sex act will do. You want something daring and extreme.

Where there is risk, there is excitement. So it makes sense that high-risk adventures would automatically be more exciting to you daredevil types. These escapades give a whole new meaning to "unsafe sex." Try them at your own risk.

944 **T**RY COMPLETELY SILENT SEX—ONCE IN A
WHILE. True, most people generally don't like dead
silence during sex (having a too-quiet partner is a top
complaint, especially among men). But to give things
a change of pace, try going an entire encounter without talking—or even making any sound at all. This
encourages eye contact and nonverbal communication and really lets you concentrate on all the physical
sensations.

945 **G**IVE SOMEONE A FREE SHOW. Stand in front of
the window topless or nude and flash someone. (Note:
This is generally only something you should do if you
live in a big city where you are surrounded by tall buildings with lots of apartments inhabited by strangers you
will most likely never meet. It's not such a good idea if
you live in the suburbs and are flashing the neighbor
you chat with every morning.)

946 **G**IVE THEM AN EVEN BETTER FREE SHOW.
Take it to the next level—have sex in front of that window.

947 **C**HECK OUT THE DRAG QUEENS. Watch a drag
show with your partner.

948 **J**UMP ONSTAGE DURING A DRAG QUEEN
SHOW. If you're brave enough, they'll probably
encourage you to show off a few moves.

949 **H**EAD TO A GAY BAR, EVEN IF YOU'RE STRAIGHT. It'll be educational and a lot of fun—and will spark up your relationship too.

950 **G**ET A **B**RAZILIAN. Yes, it is excruciatingly painful. But it will feel oh-so-freeing. And your partner will love it.

951 **G**ET A COOL DESIGN. Instead of getting completely shaved, have your hair cut into a heart or other design. Then let your partner discover your little surprise.

952 **M**AKE YOUR OWN HAIR PRODUCT FROM BODY FLUIDS. Try to re-enact the hair gel scene from *There's Something About Mary.*

953 **H**AVE SOME EROTIC PIE. Try to re-enact the pie scene from *American Pie.*

954 **L**ADIES, TRY A STRAP-ON. This is your chance to finally know how the other half lives.

955 **G**UYS, LET YOUR LADY USE A STRAP-ON ON YOU. Supposedly, one the top fantasies among women is to be a man for a day, and experience sex from their point of view. This is about as close as your partner can get to actually trading places with you in bed.

956 **DO IT IN A CHURCH.** Some couples find this very challenging and exciting . . . except for that whole eternal damnation part, which can be kind of a downer. On the bright side, you can still confess all your dirty deeds afterwards while they are still fresh in your mind.

957 **BE EXHIBITIONISTS WITH AN AUDIENCE.** Really want to take the plunge as exhibitionists? Visit a swinger club, and go at it—while leaving the door open just a crack. This is "swinger code" meaning voyeurs are welcome to watch your fun and games, but cannot come in unless invited.

958 **BE VOYEURS SEEKING A SHOW (AND MAYBE MORE).** Likewise, if you like to watch others get it on, a swinger club can be a dream come true. Remember to follow the rules, though—don't enter a cracked door unless invited. Be warned: No matter how firm your resolve is beforehand that you will "just watch," once you actually see everyone having sex around you, it can be tough to resist an invitation to join them.

959 **JOIN A SWINGER CLUB AND PARTICIPATE IN "SOFT SWINGING."** Soft swinging is a situation in which you and your partner can engage in petting, foreplay, and oral sex with other people, but not intercourse or penetration.

960 JOIN A SWINGER CLUB, AND GO ALL THE WAY. This is where you take the full plunge—having sex with other people and letting your partner do the same. Jealousy is a big risk with this idea, so be sure you (and your relationship) can handle it.

961 JOIN AN S&M CLUB. Sure, lots of people enjoy casual S&M once in a while. But now you will be playing with people who take this stuff seriously.

962 HIRE A PROFESSIONAL DOMINATRIX TO SERVE YOU ON A REGULAR BASIS. Not only can this get expensive, it can also be exhausting (not to mention painful). Proceed with caution!

963 GET A TATTOO. No, not while you're having sex (that might be a bit too risky). But many people claim to experience a rush of endorphins while getting a tattoo, putting them in an erotic state of mind. Tattoo fans often experience the best sex of their lives right after getting inked.

964 GET A SEXY TATTOO. Up the ante by getting a risqué tattoo, or getting inked in a hidden place only your special someone can see.

965 GET TATTOOED TOGETHER. For maximum effect, you can get inked at the same time as your partner, and bask in the mutual afterglow.

966 GET A FAKE, BUT PRETEND IT'S REAL. Not brave enough to go through with the real thing? Get a fake tattoo—but let your partner think it's permanent for a while. ♥

967 USE HOT WAX. The risk involved here is pretty obvious. It's hot. It's wax. And it will be near very sensitive areas. It's enough to strike sheer terror into the hearts of most people, but fans say it's incredibly erotic when used carefully. Of course, there is also the risk that you will accidentally burn the house down—and how would you explain that to your insurance company? ♥♥♥

968 LADIES, get a g-spot injection. Botox parties are so yesterday. Instead, go to a g-shot party. ♥

969 GET YOUR BELLYBUTTON PIERCED. This type of piercing is generally only sexy on ladies. ♥

970 GET YOUR NIPPLE(S) PIERCED. This is not for wimps. ♥♥

971 GET A PIERCING ON OR NEAR YOUR PRIVATE PARTS. This is pretty hardcore, but its fans claim it actually enhances the sexual experience (for both partners). ♥♥

972 GET YOUR TONGUE PIERCED. Some people swear by the thrill it adds to all kinds of sex acts. ♥♥♥

973 DO SOMETHING DANGEROUS TOGETHER. Bungee jump, skydive, or go whitewater rafting. The adrenaline can quickly spill over into sexual desire.

974 DO SOMETHING DANGEROUS TOGETHER— NAKED. This will require a bit more planning and effort. Naked bungee jumping isn't something you can do at the local county fair.

975 RISK PUBLIC EMBARRASSMENT. Dare each other do to some high-risk (or at least highly embarrassing) stunts in public. You'll feel like a team with the whole world laughing at you!

976 LET YOUR PARTNER SHAVE YOU—DOWN THERE. But don't even think about doing this if he is the slightest bit mad at you.

977 SHAVE YOUR PARTNER'S INTIMATE AREAS. Return the favor.

978 ENGAGE IN UNSAFE SEX—LITERALLY. Have unprotected sex with a new partner. This is really high-risk—to the point of being just plain dumb. Oh, and it's also possibly life-threatening.

979 ENGAGE IN UNPROTECTED SEX WITH A LONG-TERM PARTNER—DURING HER FERTILE TIME. This is totally risky for an entirely different reason. Unless you are ready for parenthood, you would need to be crazy to risk this. 💗💗💗

980 **PAY SOMEONE FOR SEX.** This is risky in all sorts of ways, especially if you do it without your partner's knowledge. 💗💗💗💗💗

981 **PAY SOMEONE FOR SEX—WITH YOU AND YOUR PARTNER.** This is less risky because your partner knows about it. However, there is still that whole pesky issue of it being against the law in most places. 💗💗💗

982 **ENJOY A BLACKOUT.** It's like having one big blindfold for both of you. You can also take advantages of having those lit candles nearby—use the wax to drip, tease, and melt each other in just the right places. 💗💗💗

983 **INDULGE YOUR SEEDY SIDE.** If you're out in the car together—running errands, carpooling home from work, on your way to the in-laws—and see a cheap motel, stop for a quickie. This isn't time for making love. Go in, do it hard and fast, and leave. Don't clean up afterward. It's okay to feel a little dirty. 💗💗💗

984 **HAVE A SPONTANEOUS DOWN-AND-DIRTY NOONER.** Surprise him with a call at work and tell him to meet you at home for a quickie. Make it fast and passionate—don't bother undressing all the way.

Just throw him down on the floor and use him up. Let him do the same to you. Straighten up your clothes, untangle your hair, and head back to work.

985 **BE A CROSS-DRESSER.** Men, try on some of your partner's clothes—perhaps a thong or a frilly dress.

986 **SECRETLY CROSS-DRESS IN PUBLIC.** Wear some of your partner's lingerie underneath your normal (manly) clothing.

987 **OPENLY CROSS-DRESS IN PUBLIC.** You can do it out of town, where nobody knows you.

988 **TAKE PART IN A GANG BANG.** This idea is perfect for people who don't want to carry all the load. There's much less pressure to perform when you're part of a group ensemble.

989 **JOIN A BUNCH OF JERKOFFS.** Attend a masturbation party. Generally, there is no touching (of other people) allowed, so it's like having sex in public in a somewhat safe environment.

990 **HOST YOUR OWN ORGY.** Only invite people that you and/or your partner find attractive. You are both guaranteed to have a good time.

991 **TRY VIAGRA.** See if it lives up to the hype.

992 TRY ONE OF THOSE MALE ENHANCEMENT CREAMS/PILLS. Enlists your partner's help in "measuring" the results.

993 HAVE (OR GIVE) A GOLDEN SHOWER. This is where you pee on your partner as part of foreplay. Yes, there are people who find this exciting (including, reportedly, a few celebrities). People usually do it in the shower for ease of cleanup.

994 ADOPT A FETISH. Fetishes seem like fun, so you have probably sometimes wished you had one. Never fear—there are plenty to choose from. Just do an online search for "fetish" and you will have enough research material to keep you busy for days.

995 EMBRACE THE FETISH YOU ALREADY HAVE. Join a club with other people who share your fetish. Subscribe to a few magazines devoted to it.

996 ENGAGE IN A LONG-TERM THREESOME. Anyone can have a one-night-stand threesome. To really show some spunk, invite your third party to move in with you, or at least set up an ongoing relationship. This is like a "plural relationship." If you thought it was tough being in a relationship with one person, wait until you try keeping two people happy on a regular basis.

997 ATTEND AN ADULT INDUSTRY CONVENTION. Upside: You'll be surrounded by porn and lots of sexy, uninhibited people. Downside: These people are hard-core freaks. Next to them, you are sure to seem boring in comparison.

998 **HAVE SEX WITH YOUR PARTNER WHILE SHE'S HAVING HER PERIOD.** Many guys find this unappealing—especially if your partner tends to be bitchy and a bit scary during this hormonal time. But some like it, so give it a shot.

999 **VISIT A NUDE BEACH.** Warning: This may sound sexier than it actually is. Most likely this beach will be open to everyone—not just the pretty people with hot bodies.

1000 **MOVE TO A NUDIST COLONY.** This is a really big step. All nudity, all the time.

1001 **TAKE THE PLUNGE, AGAIN.** Renew your vows or commitment to your partner in front of a crowd.

RESOURCES

Here's a short list of some online resources to help further your quest for sexual escapades!

Sexperts

Dr. Krista Bloom—sex and relationship coach/counselor
www.healingcouch.com

Dr. Ava Cadell—speaker, love guru, and author of several books on sex and relationships
www.loveologyuniversity.com

Paul Joannides—author of *Guide to Getting It On*
www.goofyfootpress.com

Mark Michaels—Tantric sex instructor
www.tantrapm.com

Mary Jo Fay—sex and relationship coach
www.outoftheboxx.com

Adult Films and Toys

Adam and Eve
www.adamandeve.com

Candida Royalle
www.candidaroyalle.com

Cleo's Boutique
www.cleosboutique.com

Slumber Parties by Dana
www.slumberpartiesbydana.com

Adult Games

www.fantasyplayingcards.com
www.areyougame.com
www.boardgames.com